VIDEO GAME MANIA!

MILLIONS OF PEOPLE PLAY THEM...
BILLIONS OF DOLLARS ARE SPLURGED...
AND NOW, THE REVOLUTIONARY 7-STEP
METHOD TO IMPROVE YOUR SCORES ON THE
HOTTEST NEW GAMES OF THE FANTASTIC
COMPUTER AGE!

HOW TO MASTER
THE VIDEO GAMES
BY TOM HIRSCHFELD

HOW TO MASTER THE VIDEO GAMES

by
Tom Hirschfeld

Originated by
Roberta Grossman
and
Walter Zacharius

BANTAM BOOKS
Toronto   New York   London   Sydney

HOW TO MASTER THE VIDEO GAMES

A Bantam Book / November 1981
Originated by Roberta Grossman and Walter Zacharius

ASTRO BLASTER, ASTRO FIGHTER, MOON CRESTA, SPACE FURY, SPACE ODYSSEY and MONACO GP are Trademarks of Sega Enterprises, Inc.

CENTIPEDE, ASTEROIDS, ASTEROIDS DELUXE, SKY RAIDER, BAT-TLEZONE, and MISSILE COMMAND are Trademarks of Atari, Inc.

GALAXIAN, GORF, PAC-MAN, RALLY-X, WIZARD OF WOR and SPACE ZAP are Trademarks of Midway Manufacturing Co.

PHOENIX and PLEIADES are Trademarks of Centuri, Inc.

SPACE INVADERS and SPACE INVADERS PART II are Trademarks of Taito America Corp.

DEFENDER is a Trademark of Williams Electronics, Inc.

SCRAMBLE and BERZERK are Trademarks of Stern Electronics, Inc.

STAR CASTLE and ARMOR ATTACK are Trademarks of Cinematronics, Inc.

TARG and VENTURE are Trademarks of Exidy, Inc.

CRAZY CLIMBER is a Trademark of Nichibutsu U.S.A. Corp.

Cover photograph by Bill Cadge

ISBN 0-553-20164-6

Published simultaneously in the United States and Canada

Bantam Books are published by Bantam Books, Inc. Its trademark, consisting of the words ''Bantam Books'' and the portrayal of a rooster, is Registered in U.S. Patent and Trademark Office and in other countries. Marca Registrada. Bantam Books, Inc., 666 Fifth Avenue, New York, New York 10103.

PRINTED IN THE UNITED STATES OF AMERICA

0 9 8 7 6 5 4 3 2 1

My thanks to Leo Daniels, Greg Davies, John Epstein, Sydney Gruson, Bill Heinman, Julie Herman, Alan Hirschfeld, John Hirschfeld, Leonard Hirschfeld, Phyllis Hirschfeld, Stan McEntire, Wayne McLemore, Al Michaels, Ben Roberts, Rick Scott, and Ray Tilley, and to Walter and Roberta, without whom this book could never have appeared on the screen.

CONTENTS

INTRODUCTION

Video games are not a fad.

The average machine collects about $150 per week, and hundreds of thousands of machines have been accepted by a very friendly population. It is estimated that over thirty million Americans have played within the last year, and the production of new machines is constantly increasing.

Since the introduction of the first home video games early last decade and SPACE INVADERS in 1978, video gaming has become firmly established as a national pastime.

Some social theorists don't like the trend; they say that the games can become a compulsion, almost an addiction; that they provide easy escapes from reality; and that they dehumanize players, decreasing vital interpersonal contact.

I don't see it that way; if someone is the type to become addicted, better to video games than to something both more expensive and more physically damaging.

Almost everyone occasionally escapes from reality in one way or another. Games seem to me one of the more harmless, even beneficial, methods.

Arcades, far from isolating players from the rest of the human race, are becoming major neighborhood social centers. They're like clubs, with members drawn together by common interests and friendly competition.

Furthermore, video games improve players' reflexes and mental powers far more than many other activities; for instance, watching today's television shows. The games offer a chance to participate, to enjoy oneself non-passively, and to release tension and aggression. In a society moving toward complete computerization, the games teach self-reliance and computer confidence.

This book explains the principles on which the games are based. An understanding of how they work can lead not only to improved technique, but to a clearer comprehension of the technology influencing our lives daily. Mainly, though, I want readers to get the scores they want.

My conversations with friends and players across the country have helped me formulate a basic approach to game learning. This approach will serve as a simple guide, a foundation for the method each person eventually finds most effective.

The thirty game strategies are more specific, each one an explanation of a particular game. The same format is used each time:

1. Diagram of the screen with all parts labeled, excluding score displays
2. Explanation of the controls
3. Explanation of the scoring system, which occasionally varies from location to location
4. Explanation of direct threats to the player–what occurrences will end the game
5. Observations about the game
6. Strategies, from the obvious to the subtle, derived from all the information above.

The games fall into five categories: SPACE INVADERS-type, ASTEROIDS-type, maze, reflex, and miscellaneous. All the SPACE INVADERS-type games confine the player's ship to an area at the bottom of the screen, whereas the ASTEROIDS-type games allow it unlimited mobility.

Machine owners, called "operators," sometimes speed up their games or otherwise modify the programs with new circuits, hoping to increase revenue by forcing the player's turn to end more quickly. This book, however, concerns the original models except where otherwise noted.

Because so many home video games operate on the same principles as their arcade counterparts, I have included a brief guide to the "other" kind of games for those interested. For players who would like to get in touch with video game manufacturers, the book concludes with a list of names, addresses, and telephone numbers.

One word before you go on: play well, but don't take the games too seriously. The purpose of all this is to enjoy yourself.

1

FOR BEGINNERS ONLY

If you are a newcomer to the world of video games, you should familiarize yourself with some of their common characteristics. Every game, for example, involves some type of maneuvering by the player, accomplished by the use of buttons or levers (known as "joysticks") or some combination of the two. After reading the Controls section of a game strategy, you will understand immediately your potential for maneuvering in that game.

Most games use one or more FIRE buttons. Except when the Observations section states differently, the player's spaceship, plane, tank, or other representative fires in the direction it is facing. In the SPACE INVADERS-type games, it always faces up. The player's enemies, when hit, explode and disappear without a trace, except as noted in CENTIPEDE, GORF, and a few other games.

The player always has an objective: scoring points. This effort usually involves shooting as many enemies or clearing as great a distance as possible. Enemies often appear in "screens" that must be annihilated before the next screen appears. Other names for screens, depending on the game, are "rounds," "missions," "sectors," "attacks," or "waves."

Games sometimes operate on large and small cycles. GORF, for instance, has five missions in every round, always in the same order; but in ASTRO BLASTER, there are six sectors in every round and at least four attacks in every sector, also in the same order every time. The names vary from game to game, but one fact holds true for all games: the better you play them, the harder they get.

2

KNOW YOUR ENEMY

A video games expert doesn't have to be a computer whiz, but a rudimentary understanding of a machine's insides never hurts if you want to rule the outside. When you are analyzing the way a game thinks, you should know at least a little about the form of its brain.

In the following diagram, "input" refers to your actions at the controls; what you do is relayed instantly to tiny silicon chips known as microprocessors. The machine uses two types of recall, Random Access Memory (RAM) and Read Only Memory (ROM). The RAM retains temporary data, such as your score, the number of ships you have left, and the day's high scores. The ROM, however, never alters; it keeps permanent information such as the rules of the game—that is, the program, which is usually written in assembler language.

Almost every program uses a Random Event Generator (REG). The REG prevents you from predicting when and where your next enemy will appear, for example, or how much the next mystery ship will be worth.

So, your actions are fed into the microprocessors, which use them plus the RAM and ROM to produce the output that appears on the screen microseconds later.

The screen is usually like an ordinary television monitor, with black-and-white or color images. The graphics can be achieved through one of two systems: raster, in which thousands of tiny dots change hue separately to alter the picture, or vector, in which the machine actually draws images with straight lines. Color vector graphics are the rarest type. Part of the program also produces the "attract mode," which appears on the screen when no one is playing, often including the initials of the day's high scorers.

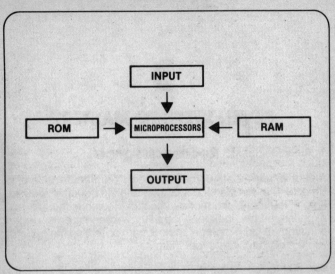

The more you know about how games "think," the better you can analyze and master any game.

3

SEVEN STEPS TO MASTERY

1. Reconnaissance

A quarter spent before you have seen the attract mode and at least five sample bouts of a game is a quarter wasted. Before you spend any money, you should watch other players, experienced and inexperienced. From observing other beginners, you will learn a game's pitfalls; from observing the experts, you will learn how to avoid them.

It is an unfortunate fact that most players are better suited for some types of games than for others. If you run up against a game you are not able to improve in and do not genuinely enjoy, don't be ashamed to abandon it. It's easier to become good at a game you enjoy; entertainment and proficiency are, after all, the two basic goals in video gaming.

2. Teamwork

Once you have selected a game to try, you need a friend. Even aside from two-player cooperative games such as WIZARD OF WOR, game mastery at its best is very much a team effort.

You should rely on your friend to take notes during experiments (see Step 6), to supply advice and constructive criticism, and to provide a foil for your own comments and insights. He or she will be able to observe a game's workings objectively without the pressure of playing it.

Encourage your friend and compare impressions with him; when you tell him your ideas, you will both enlighten him and make the ideas clearer in your own mind. Teamwork will always help more than it hurts.

4

3. Concentration

When you are learning a difficult video game, you should not be thinking about Bar-B-Q-flavored potato chips. You must learn to channel your attention into the new world you have entered, be it outer space, undersea, or elsewhere.

The off-machine exercises discussed in Chapter 9 will train you to devote less mental energy to the mechanics of the game. Once you are comfortable with the controls, you can attain the most precious single attribute of an expert–confidence.

Confidence allows you not only to operate the controls automatically but even to make simple strategic decisions automatically. A MISSILE COMMAND master can know without conscious thought that he has destroyed one missile, although he is already moving on to three more. Confidence transforms the intermediate player into the expert and can be reached only through concentration.

4. Tempo

Even before your first attempt at a game, try to get a feeling for its rhythms (see Chapter 9). Once you have unconsciously absorbed knowledge of the "heartbeat" of a machine, the inevitable timing and patterns will all begin to fall into place.

Each program works in established chronological intervals, which you can learn almost without effort. Once you understand a rhythm, taking advantage of it through synchronization and/or syncopation can be quite simple and will produce fantastic results.

5. Observation

If you see something happen on the screen, remember it. It happened because some detail in the software made it happen; understanding and remembering that detail will certainly help you in the future.

The next five chapters are filled with my own observations and those of other players. You will have to make similar ones for mastery of any game you choose to learn.

6. Experimentation

When you have the impression that some sequence of appearances or point values is not altogether random, experimentation will pay dividends. If it turns out you were wrong, you lose a quarter; if you were right, your whole approach to the game can change for the better.

The most famous case of successful experimentation was the quest for the 300-point UFO in SPACE INVADERS (see next chapter). Perhaps no one player discovered the secret, but it is a secret no more; practically every half-serious player knows it. The technique's tremendous impact on all strategy and attack sequences is a measure of the value of the method by which it was devised. The secret bonuses in ASTRO BLASTER can be discovered the same way and with similar results.

7. Memorization

The awful truth is that some games without REGs, such as PAC-MAN and SCRAMBLE, have definite patterns that you must memorize for optimum performance. You can accomplish much by familiarity with the mechanics and controls of a game but, for true virtuosity, you need a complete understanding of its inner workings. And so, you must memorize.

Whether you have a photographic memory or one like a sieve, you can find a way to remember what is necessary. Your training partner can jot down important numbers or positions while you play, or you can imprint them on your memory when playing.

Once you have used reconnaissance, teamwork, concentration, tempo, observation, experimentation, and memorization on the game of your choice, you will find that the accomplishment has placed mastery within your reach without lessening the excitement or the challenge for an instant.

4

SPACE INVADERS-
TYPE GAMES

1. ASTRO BLASTER

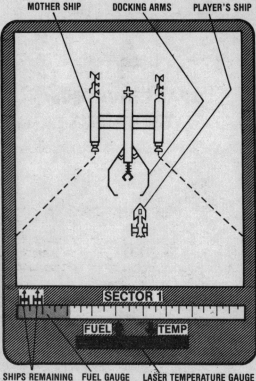

MOTHER SHIP   DOCKING ARMS   PLAYER'S SHIP

SECTOR 1

FUEL   TEMP

SHIPS REMAINING   FUEL GAUGE   LASER TEMPERATURE GAUGE
(Non-Functional during Docking)

CONTROLS

a. Left and right directional buttons

b. FIRE button

c. WARP button

SCORING

a. Meteor: 100 points

8

b. Enemy ship: 50-250 points, depending on size and speed

c. Various secret bonuses (see Observation i)

DANGERS

a. if the player's ship is shot or rammed by any enemy ship, it is destroyed.

b. if the player's ship is hit by a meteor or fireball, it is destroyed.

c. if the player runs out of fuel, crashes during docking, or loses all his ships, the game ends.

OBSERVATIONS

a. ASTRO BLASTER challenges the player with an amazing 29 different attacks, distributed through six sectors. Each succeeding sector has more difficult attacks, and more of them.

After the sixth sector, the game repeats itself. Between sectors, the player is subjected to a meteor shower, then given a chance to dock.

Attacks involve four or more enemy ships—different in shape and color with each attack—that may travel vertically, horizontally, diagonally, evasively, or in some combination of styles. Everything occurs in a predetermined order.

b. The player's ship moves along the bottom of the screen and can have any number of shots in the air at a time.

c. The player begins each sector with a new fuel supply. The fuel is consumed as time passes, not as a result of maneuvering or shooting. When the fuel is reduced to a certain level, the machine's voice synthesizer announces, "Fuel status marginal."

d. Next comes, "Fuel status critical. Use extreme caution." After this warning, only nine seconds elapse before the fuel runs out and the game ends. And now for the good news: every object you shoot during Fuel Status Critical scores double points.

e. Meteor showers occur just before docking, when fuel is lowest. Meteors and fireballs streak down the screen; the latter are more valuable than the former. When fireballs are hit, they supply three seconds' worth of fuel each. If the player can survive until docking, he has it made, especially since he receives a bonus for fuel remaining.

f. If the player fires too frequently for too long, the machine warns, "Laser temperature critical." If the shooting continues, the ship temporarily loses its ability to fire. Both the laser temperature and the fuel are constantly monitored at the bottom of the screen.

g. When the player presses WARP, the machine's voice reacts. "Warp activated. 10, 9, 8, 7. . ." Everything on the screen but the player's ship slows almost to a standstill, even if the countdown spans two attacks.

When it reaches 1, the machine warns the player that everything is about to return to normal velocity, at least five times greater than warp speed. Then the action resumes at the usual speed, and the player cannot use WARP again with the same ship in the same sector.

h. In docking, the player uses his directional buttons to avoid crashing. Once the ship has docked, it receives a full tank of fuel and a bonus for fuel remaining. Then the next sector commences.

i. Here are some of the game's secret bonuses:

3–1,000 points for shooting without missing throughout Fuel Status Marginal

4–700 points for demolishing an entire horizontal attack before it can reach the right edge of the screen

9–400–1,500 points for accuracy in docking without using the buttons at all; also, 1,500 by the "paint-scraper" bonus, given for brushing against one of the docking arms

13–700 points for finding the right sequence in which to shoot any attack (left to right, top to bottom, etc.)

15–1,500 points for shooting any Sector Three attack in order

16–2,000 points for shooting the amoebas in Sector Four as they appear at top; when two appear at once, the player must hit the left one first

22–600 points for going through an entire sector without hitting Laser Temperature Critical

25–500 points for keeping a ship through an entire sector

The rest of the bonuses are set along the same lines.

STRATEGIES

a. Learn the sequences of the game to avoid nasty surprises, such as destruction by a sudden diagonal attack. These fast-moving attacks can appear as close as three inches from your ship.

b. Experiment to learn more about the game, especially the secret bonuses. Your scores will increase as your knowledge increases.

c. Don't waste time near the beginning of a sector unless you want to run out of fuel near the end.

d. If you are confident in your shooting skill, let yourself enter Fuel Status Critical just before each meteor shower. You can survive on the fuel gained by hitting fireballs, while reaping double points for hitting meteors. Just watch the fuel gauge and don't let yourself get too low.

If you do, press WARP to slow down the fireballs you need to shoot. If you have used up your warp for that ship and sector, you are in trouble. Your only choice is to crash the ship and press WARP as soon as you get the next. Fuel is more important than individual ships in ASTRO BLASTER.

e. Learn to fire effectively but not constantly for two reasons: you will always have laser when you need it, and you will have chances for Secret Bonuses #3 and #22 and others.

f. Since you can press WARP only once per ship per sector, try to save it for the most difficult attacks, such as the horizontal ones. In addition to saving time, you will also earn Secret Bonus #4.

g. Learn to dock smoothly before you try for the paint-scraper bonus. If you accustom yourself to the ship's relative vertical and horizontal speeds during docking, you will avert needless crashes.

While the meteor shower diminishes, move your ship to center for the "hands off" bonus, #9.

h. The secret bonuses help to make ASTRO BLASTER unusual and exciting. Learn them and, fuel permitting, go for them.

2. ASTRO FIGHTER

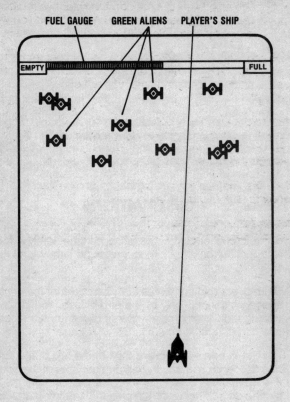

FUEL GAUGE   GREEN ALIENS   PLAYER'S SHIP

EMPTY   FULL

CONTROLS

a. Left and right directional buttons

b. FIRE button

SCORING

a. Blue alien: 20 points

b. Purple alien: 30 points

c. Green alien: 40 points

13

d. Yellow alien: 50 points

e. "GS" alien: 300-1,000 points

f. Light bulb: 60 points

DANGERS

a. Collision with any of the aliens or their missiles destroys the player's ship.

b. Collision with any light bulb does the same.

c. When the player loses all his ships or runs out of fuel, the game ends.

OBSERVATIONS

a. The player's ship can have only one missile on the screen at a time and does not always respond immediately to the directional buttons. When it does respond, it moves relatively slowly.

b. The player's ship consumes fuel at a constant rate, able to replenish its supply only at the end of each round. On the average, destroying one wave of aliens consumes about one-fifth of a tankful.

c. The first four waves of aliens start at the top of the screen and descend gradually. If even one escapes at the bottom, the wave starts over in full force at the top, with the ship placed an inch higher on the screen. If the ship is destroyed in the middle of a wave, however, only the remaining attackers start at the top to confront its replacement.

d. Light bulbs descend slowly in straight lines during the first four waves, providing a hindrance to the player's movements and a few extra points. (I thought at first that hitting one might add to the fuel supply, but it doesn't.)

e. The aliens launch missiles randomly, both diagonally and straight down. The diagonal ones are much harder to dodge.

f. The first wave contains 15 blue aliens stacked in a 5-4-3-2-1 pyramid. The long bottom edge extends across half the screen, and the formation can appear anywhere along the top edge. Once they are on the screen, the blue aliens descend in a quick knitting-needle pattern (down-over-up-over-down, with down strokes the longest).

g. The second wave's 15 purple aliens descend in the same style as their blue predecessors, but they are deployed in two long rows across the screen.

h. The green aliens in the third wave descend in a markedly different fashion and in random formation. Each one descends to the right or left at a 45° angle. Once it stops, it can move in only one direction: the one from which it came. Then it stops again somewhere along the line and descends at a 45° angle in the other direction.

It usually descends farther than it ascends, producing a tricky downward trend, but it might touch the bottom of the screen and then ascend twice before finally escaping if the player permits. The green aliens' erratic movements make them the most formidable of the five types of attackers.

i. The fourth wave's aliens, on the other hand, seem to be the easiest. They descend straight in five close-set columns of three, with one or two columns starting half an inch below the others. They do, however, descend much more rapidly than any of their predecessors.

j. In the fifth wave, a single alien roams the top third of the screen. It resembles an ornate picture frame with the letters GS (Gremlin/Sega) at center. Launching only a few missiles at the player's ship, the alien presents an easy target that is worth more the farther away it is hit.

The shot must hit the alien's center, though, and the player can fire only through the gap in the middle of a funnel-like structure that stretches across the screen throughout the attack. Once the alien is destroyed, it refills the player's fuel tank.

STRATEGIES

a. Shoot whenever you have a target, as in most SPACE IN-VADERS-type games. To shoot at as many targets as possible, follow two simple rules:

1. As soon as one shot detonates, fire the next if there's anything to hit. If not, the second rule applies.

2. Start shifting under the next target even before the first blows up. If it turns out that you missed, you can always go back. You should seldom miss on the first try once you know how your enemy moves.

b. Dispatch your adversaries as quickly as you can; otherwise, an empty fuel tank will end the game prematurely.

c. If you have lost no ships and a single escaping alien is jeopardizing your fuel supply—you can't afford to start a whole wave over—block its path no matter what, sacrificing one ship to help yourself survive the round.

d. Avoid being blocked by falling light bulbs, but shoot them only if there is no more urgent need for missiles; for instance, when crossing the screen to attack or in the lull between waves.

e. Beware of diagonal missiles, trying never to put yourself in a vulnerable position (see Strategies f and g).

f. Shoot the pyramid of blue invaders from the bottom up. If you eliminate the bottom two rows fast enough, you will not be threatened by diagonal missiles.

g. Shoot both ends of the purple formation first to avoid being plagued by diagonal shots once you are close and have less time to dodge them. With the ends gone, eliminate the three or four lower attackers in the middle section, then finish off the upper tier.

h. Once you know the green aliens' patterns, you can usually pick off five or six in a row without even moving. To select the right spot, look for a cluster of them at the beginning of their attack. Remember, however, that once you do move, each attacker can reverse direction at any moment; very

rarely does one travel more than three inches without doing so. And don't despair if you see one exit at the bottom,
since you have at least two more shots at it before its exit
from the screen.

i. Shooting quickly to demolish one column at a time, the
    lower ones first, should end the fourth wave smoothly.

j. Wait until the GS alien seems about to reach its highest
    point before firing. You can wait as long as your fuel holds
    out, but don't forget to dodge the few missiles that the alien
    does fire.

    If you move to center and start shooting as soon as you
    complete the fourth wave, you will sometimes catch your
    enemy by surprise all the way at the top of the screen, net-
    ting at least 900 points.

k. After the first round, you will notice that ships become even
    scarcer than fuel, so you must exercise even more caution
    with them.

3. CENTIPEDE

BODY SEGMENTS

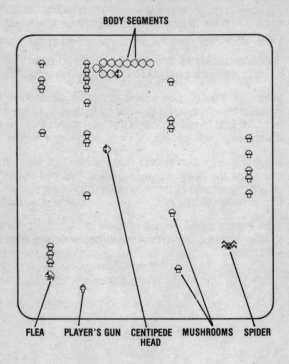

FLEA   PLAYER'S GUN   CENTIPEDE   MUSHROOMS   SPIDER
HEAD

CONTROLS

a. Trak-Ball

b. FIRE button

SCORING

a. Mushroom totally destroyed: 1 point

b. Centipede body segment: 10 points

c. Centipede head: 100 points

d. Flea: 200 points

18

e. Spider: 300, 600, or 900 points

f. Scorpion: 1,000 points

g. Bonus whenever player's gun is destroyed (see Observation k).

h. Bonus gun every 12,000 points

DANGERS

a. Collision with any centipede, flea, or spider destroys the player's gun.

OBSERVATIONS

a. With Atari's Trak-Ball, the player can instantly maneuver anywhere in the bottom three inches of the screen.

b. A player can have only one bullet in the air at a time, but keeping the FIRE button down insures that a bullet is fired the instant the last one detonates. When the target is close, the effect is "rapid-fire." The gun fires only straight upward.

c. It takes four shots to shoot away any mushroom. The mushrooms are not directly lethal to the player, but they do block his movements.

d. All the denizens of the mushroom patch except the player can operate on either of two speeds; in early rounds, all travel slowly. More and more new centipedes then start out fast until they all do; fleas can shift gears in midflight; spiders all go fast after about 10,000 points; and scorpions switch to fast after about 15,000.

e. Each centipede appears at top left, traveling to the right. It is composed of a head and up to 11 body segments, which trail after it. The centipede always travels from side to side except when it strikes a mushroom or the side of the screen; then it descends one level—even if that means passing through a mushroom from the top—and heads off in the opposite direction. There are about 30 levels on the screen; if the mushrooms are set close enough, the centipedes will zigzag down more than they travel across.

When the player shoots a centipede in the head, it turns into a mushroom, and the next segment becomes the head. If the player shoots a body segment, the segment becomes a mushroom, and the centipede splits in two opposite directions, with the tail end sprouting eyes to become a head.

If the player shoots a descending centipede, the first part hit will turn into a mushroom, but the others—since they are not coming from the side—will not stop and can be shot one by one with rapid-fire as they come. The whole process leaves only one or two mushrooms, which then can be shot away in a second.

f. Spiders are confined to the same area as the player and can travel only vertically or diagonally. They appear at the top left or top right corner of the player's zone; from the moment of their appearance, they cannot turn back, although they can bounce up and down without traveling sideways.

Each spider must be destroyed or exit from the opposite edge of the screen before the next can appear. When they zigzag across the screen, they rebound off the top and bottom borders of the zone, off centipedes, and off mushrooms, or in midair. The spider erases all the mushrooms it touches, but the player receives no points for mushrooms thus destroyed.

A spider's value increases as it moves closer to the player. When a spider is destroyed in a collision with the gun, however, the player gets no points.

g. Only one flea can be on the screen at a time. They appear continuously as long as there are fewer than five mushrooms in the player's zone.

Falling straight from the top of the screen, fleas leave a random number of mushrooms in the zone in a column behind them. Fleas are direct threats to the player only if he is under them and has no time to shoot, but the mushrooms they leave behind can cause him trouble (see Observation i).

h. Scorpions appear one at a time and travel in a straight line across the screen, moving to the left or right somewhere above the player's zone, often too high for him to have a clear shot at them. As they cross, they poison a row of mushrooms.

If poison mushrooms are too high for the player to touch, how can they be dangerous? This is how: as soon as a centipede hits the side of a poison mushroom, it rushes pell-mell to the bottom of the screen, not stopping its narrow zigzag until its head is shot or it reaches the second-to-bottom level, where it turns to the right or the left, regaining normal movement.

i. As soon as all the centipedes on the screen have reached the bottom row, the machine releases one new head from the top left or top right corner of the player's zone every five seconds until the player either clears the screen or loses his gun. After a few heads have been released and not killed, the machine begins sending them out every three seconds, then every two seconds, then every second, making survival increasingly improbable, since scorpions, fleas, and spiders are all simultaneously pursuing their appointed rounds.

Once any centipede, whether it has 1 or 12 segments, reaches the bottom level, it rises again to the top of the player's zone and starts down again, using its standard mode of locomotion both ways. It is therefore undesirable to have mushrooms cluttering up the zone, since they accelerate each journey the centipedes make. If the zone is not cleared soon enough, the player must lose his gun sooner or later.

j. Each of the player's enemies has its own sound effect, beginning the instant it appears.

k. Whenever a gun is destroyed, the machine repairs all the partially-shot and poison mushrooms, giving the player a bonus of 5 points for each one.

l. When the first, twelve-segmented centipede is finished off, all the colors on the screen change and the next round begins. An eleven-segmented and a one-segmented centipede appear; once they are dispatched, a ten-segmented and two one-segmented ones appear; and so

on until the twelfth round, which begins with twelve heads.
The thirteenth round starts with one long centipede in high
gear, and the same pattern is repeated. Segments are, of
course, more difficult to destroy separately than all at once.

STRATEGIES

a. Remember, never stay still. Get as close as you can to whatever you shoot, so you can fire again right away.

b. A common mistake that most beginners make is to use
   nothing but rapid-fire; thus, they have less control of timing
   than the sophisticated player who removes his finger from
   the FIRE button. If you shoot indiscriminately, you might find
   yourself unable to fire when you have to. In CENTIPEDE, you
   want to take as few chances as possible.

c. Always clear your zone of mushrooms, especially columns
   near the sides, where centipedes will reach the bottom
   very quickly by rushing down between the column and the
   edge.

   Also, learn to recognize which mushroom formations will
   make centipedes turn, so you can use rapid-fire on them as
   they do turn.

d. Since everything runs on two speeds, prevent mistiming by
   recognizing when an enemy speeds up or slows down.

e. When a centipede is descending towards you, try to hit its
   head first for two reasons:

   1. You will earn 100 points instead of 10, and the head will
      immediately be replaced.

   2. You will keep the centipede in one piece. The strategy of
      "divide and conquer" does **not** apply to CENTIPEDE.

f. Sometimes, a long string of segments will pass over you to
   the left or right. You should do one of the following:

   1. Speed over to where you know it will turn and get your
      rapid-fire ready.

   2. Sweep under the whole centipede with the FIRE button

down. You must move toward the head, not away from it, or else the first mushroom you create will make the rest of the centipede turn, crashing down onto you. This method, if you judge your speed right, will destroy nearly the whole beast.

g. Stay away from the edges whenever a spider is not on the screen. The reason for this is that you never know when or from which top corner one will emerge. Learn to predict spiders' rebounds; one common misfortune is for a spider to bounce off the top, off the bottom, off a centipede's underside, and onto the bewildered player.

Once you are conscious of the spider's location, you can move to the other side of it and know that you are safe, since it cannot reverse its lateral motion. Whenever you have time, though, you should blast it, since spiders are your greatest potential source of points, and points give you more guns. For maximum score, move as close as you safely can before you shoot.

h. Shoot fleas whenever you have the time, both for points and to spare yourself from having to clean up after them. That is one example of a time when you must save your shots to be sure you'll have one ready before the flea can crush you. The worst fleas are those that fall close together; the two columns they leave form a perfect channel for centipedes.

i. Go after the scorpions only when you have a clear shot at them; once a scorpion has crossed, be ready for a long centipede to hit a poison mushroom and come twisting down. Zap it before it gets too far.

j. When the last segments of a screen reach your zone, shoot them before the machine can send in more. If it's only one head, let it get almost to the bottom before you kill it, meanwhile shooting a few mushrooms and spiders while you have the chance.

Wait for a head to cross over you before you shoot it; your aim will be better if you are still. Beware, however, of the following mistake: beginners often reflexively rise into the head as they shoot it, committing inadvertent suicide.

Keep in mind that two heads colliding will both descend and turn away. Anticipate this and dodge in time.

k. Listen for sound effects to know when you're threatened: two senses are better than one. Sound effects are especially useful in detecting fleas and scorpions.

l. If you fire a few shots as you cross the screen, the mushrooms you damage will yield five points each after your next demise. Use rapid-fire, then, as long as you are ready to shoot when you must.

m. As the game progresses, ignore minor concerns and concentrate on three basic priorities:

   1. Avoid immediate dangers such as spiders and fleas. Shooting is better than dodging when there's time.

   2. Keep your zone clear of mushrooms.

   3. Exterminate descending centipedes as early as possible.

4. GALAXIAN

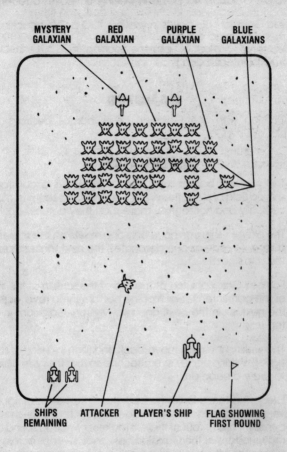

MYSTERY GALAXIAN   **RED GALAXIAN**   **PURPLE GALAXIAN**   **BLUE GALAXIANS**

SHIPS REMAINING   **ATTACKER**   **PLAYER'S SHIP**   **FLAG SHOWING FIRST ROUND**

CONTROLS

a. Left and right directional buttons

b. FIRE button

SCORING

a. Blue Galaxian: 30 points in waiting, 60 points attacking

25

b. Purple Galaxian: 40 points in waiting, 80 points attacking

c. Red Galaxian: 50 points in waiting, 100 points attacking

d. Mystery Galaxian: 60 points in waiting; 150, 200, 300, or 800 points attacking

DANGERS

a. Collision with any Galaxian or its bombs destroys the player's ship.

OBSERVATIONS

a. The screen's background is deceptive–it is a constantly shifting field of stars–therefore the Galaxians seem to move vertically and horizontally more than they actually do.

b. The player's ship can have only one missile on the screen at a time. As soon as one detonates, the next materializes at the ship's nozzle.

c. Forty-six Galaxians are at the top of the screen at the start of the game: ten in each of the bottom three rows, eight in the next, six in the next, and two Mystery Galaxians in the top row.

  The waiting invaders move back and forth in a kind of small zigzag, shifting slightly every second so that they are difficult to draw a bead on.

d. Every so often, a Galaxian from the extreme left or right inverts and attacks. Only then does it drop its needle-shaped bombs, three or four of them. It makes a whistling sound that grows louder as the Galaxian descends, sweeps across the screen, and then exits at the edge, only to reappear at the top and tumble into its original position.

e. Whenever a new screen starts, a flag appears at bottom right; so there are three flags during the third screen, six during the sixth, and so on.

f. Each Mystery Galaxian can have four different values when attacking. If one attacks alone, it is worth 150 points; with one red escort, 200; with two escorts, 300; and if the player shoots both escorts first, 800.

g. In later screens, there are more Galaxians in each screen, and up to five will attack at once, with five-second rest breaks every 30 seconds. After the tenth flag, though, there are no more rest breaks, and the player is under constant maximum bombardment. Moreover, the attackers have wider and wider suicidal sweeps lower and lower on the screen.

STRATEGIES

a. Shoot as often as possible, starting as soon as your ship materializes.

b. In order not to waste shots, learn how to shift sideways with the body of the Galaxians as you fire. The first step in learning this skill is to ignore the tricky background.

c. Shoot red Galaxians only when they are accompanying a Mystery Galaxian; shoot Mystery Galaxians only when they are attacking. By doing so, you will have a better chance of scoring 800 for each Mystery Galaxian.

d. Learn the Galaxians' attack patterns. The purple ones, for instance, fly almost across the screen, then reverse direction and exit at the bottom. They are at their most vulnerable when they are turning out of a wide sweep, since they slow down and do not drop bombs then. Follow them across the screen and shoot them at that point.

e. Always watch for an attacker's bombs, even if you have just hit the attacker itself. The one you don't see could destroy your ship.

f. If you see that an attacker will reach its most vulnerable point within one second, hold your fire until then, so that you can be sure of being able to shoot it.

Remember that each Galaxian is worth at least twice as much when attacking, so the points you gain by waiting will more than offset the time you lose, at least in the early screens.

g. When you miss an attacker or when there are too many to deal with, the right or left edge of the screen is usually a safe shelter during the early screens, but stay there no longer than you must.

5. GORF

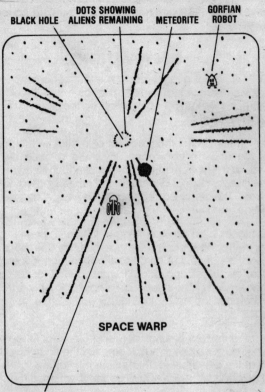

BLACK HOLE
DOTS SHOWING
ALIENS REMAINING
METEORITE
GORFIAN ROBOT
SPACE WARP
PLAYER'S SHIP

CONTROLS

a. Multidirectional joystick

b. Laser trigger in joystick

SCORING

Many different scoring values; the important ones are set forth in the observations below.

29

DANGERS

a. If the player's ship is shot or rammed by any of its enemies, it is destroyed.

OBSERVATIONS

a. GORF is unusual in that it consists of five separate missions, several of them video games in their own right. Its voice synthesizer, challenging or complimenting the player, is another distinctive feature.

b. Also different is the multidirectional joystick with its trigger. The player's ship can move anywhere within a block of space at the bottom of the screen; although it can move in an infinite number of directions and curves, it always points upward. The player can control all this motion, and fire, with just one hand.

c. The trigger is no ordinary trigger. It fires a special "quark laser" with a new touch: the player has only one shot on the screen at a time, but **he** chooses which one. If the player misses his target and doesn't want to wait for his shot to reach the top of the screen, all he has to do is press the trigger. Instantly, the first shot will disappear, and the next will be fired.

d. The missions that are not derived from established video games do have one thing in common: the enemies in them aim at the player's ship. The various missiles are fortunately not guided, so the player can dodge them once they have been fired.

e. In most missions, enemies trying to ram the player will enter his mobility zone. When some of them are shot, small numerals showing their point values appear for a second or two where the attackers were at the moment they were shot.

If the player shoots such an attacker in his own zone, he may hit the numerals themselves with his ship. If he does, his ship is destroyed.

f. Astro Battles—This first mission, similar to the game SPACE IN-

VADERS (see page 155), is relatively innocuous because there are only 24 invaders, compared to 55 in each screen of the original game. This version is like the original with a few exceptions:

1. The UFO at the top of the screen sometimes stops in its tracks and reverses direction. Whenever it is hit, it shows a value of 100 points.

2. The invaders do not appear all at once. First a large Gorfian robot, cute and pink, appears and begins dropping them into formation. None moves or shoots until all three rows of eight have been arranged and the robot has vanished.

3. If the player manages to shoot the robot, it explodes but continues its job of dropping invaders. Once they are all down, it disappears, leaving only the half-inch-high numerals which proclaim its value, 250 points.

   Smaller Gorfian robots prance across the top of the screen every now and then; they are worth 300 points each.

4. In this mission only, a white semicircle, one-quarter-inch thick, lies between the ship and the invaders. Its diameter is the width of the screen, and its endpoints are at the two bottom corners.

   It vanishes for an instant to let the player's shots pass through, but the invaders' missiles must blast holes in it. The shield serves the same function as the shelters in SPACE INVADERS, which GORF lacks. As with the shelters, any invaders that come low enough pass through it with no trouble.

5. If the player's ship is destroyed with only one or two invaders left, the mission still ends.

g. Laser Attack—The enemy forces here are centered on two laser cannons that fire simultaneously every two or three seconds. They shift vertically and horizontally all over the screen, pulling their clusters of escorts with them. They always move, stop, and then shoot. Each laser cannon is worth 300 points.

The sound effects of a laser shot are unmistakable warnings. It should be noted, though, that a shot fired just before the cannon is hit will have the same duration and deadliness as any other.

The escorts detach themselves one or two at a time and try to ram the player's ship from above without firing. If they are not destroyed but miss, they reappear at the top of the screen and fall back into place until their next attempt.

Some of the escorts are little Gorfian robots, but most are creatures resembling badminton birdies. The object of the mission is to destroy them and their cannons.

h. Galaxians—Not too different from the original game by this name, with these exceptions:

1. Instead of 46 Galaxians, as in the original's first screen, the mission begins with only 24 (two rows of eight, a row of six, and a row of two).

2. The Galaxians' bombs are no longer needles, but pellets.

3. Gorfian robots hop across the top of the screen from time to time, worth 100 points each when hit.

i. Space Warp—A black hole releases spiraling spaceships and Gorfian robots that hurl meteorites at the player's ship. The attackers emerge from the hole one at a time with a spiral motion; they increase in size until they destroy the ship, are destroyed themselves (100 points), or go off the edge.

The player's mobility zone extends higher than usual, to about two inches below the black hole; thus he can fly high enough to be hit either by the meteorites from above or by the attackers from the side.

Whenever a new attacker emerges from the black hole, the machine signals it by a sound effect and takes a dot from the string of dots around the black hole. The mission ends when the fixed number of attackers has emerged.

j. Flagship—The flagship is a large, angular vessel with a nuclear reactor in its middle. It flies slowly from side to side near the top of the screen, descending each time and dropping diamond-shaped bombs with stems.

When the player shoots the ship anywhere but the reactor, he earns 20 points and makes a hole. Sometimes, he severs one chunk from the main body, and it falls down; he can make 150 points by finishing it off. When he makes enough holes in the reactor casing to shoot through it, the whole ship explodes, giving the player 1,000 points.

A large semicircular shield, with its endpoints in the two top corners, protects the flagship until the player shoots a few holes in it. Everything falling from above passes through the shield without difficulty; thus the shield offers no protection to the player.

Nothing can hit the player's ship if it stays in the extreme upper right or left. When the flagship is finally destroyed, the next round begins, with the player one rank higher (see Observation k).

k. At the end of the first round only, the player receives one bonus ship. There are six ranks he can attain, depending on how many rounds he survives. In the first round, he is a Space Cadet; in the second, a Space Captain; in the third, a Space Colonel; in the fourth, a Space General; in the fifth, a Space Warrior; and from the sixth on, a Space Avenger.

Each round from Space Cadet to Space General is increasingly difficult, after which they remain at the same level of difficulty. Missions are numbered without regard to rounds; for instance, Astro Battles the second time around is Mission Six.

Here is a breakdown of how each mission grows more difficult with time.

1. The invaders move more quickly and shoot more often (up to four missiles on the screen at a time).

2. The laser cannons move, stop, and fire more quickly.

3. The Galaxians eventually dive-bomb the player five at a time, each attacking more viciously than ever.

4. The attackers from the black hole move much faster. When they are at the top of the screen, their meteorites fly faster than when they are nearer the player's ship.

5. After the first round, two Gorfian robots always ride on the flagship. They never fire, but they do drop down to ram the player's ship. When hit, they are worth 100 points each. The flagship, meanwhile, crosses the screen more and more quickly and begins dropping up to four bombs at a time.

STRATEGIES

a. Learn to use the controls; develop a feeling for how fast the ship moves when you pull the joystick in various directions.

b. Develop the reflex of firing again as soon as you miss a target. Speed in finishing the mission is most important in Astro Battles.

c. Keeping your ship is more important than earning maximum points, so maneuver defensively. You must keep moving to avoid the missiles aimed at you. A series of tight circles can be very effective in both offensive and defensive situations.

d. Keep away from the numerals indicating the point values of attackers you've destroyed. If you were moving upward and shot the alien pointblank, stop.

e. Shoot the large robot as it drops the first few invaders, then go into action against them. You don't need the subtlety you would for SPACE INVADERS; simply kill them off as quickly as possible, staying clear of their fire as explained in the strategies for SPACE INVADERS. You should always have time to take care of one or two robots and UFOs, as well. Learn when and where they emerge, and take the time to shoot them.

f. In Mission Two, shoot the first escort that attacks you, then shoot both laser cannons as quickly as you can. Once both are gone, the mission is easy.

The first escort is harder to shoot, since you must meanwhile watch out for the other. The best method is to dart under it just after it shoots, fire, and escape to the side. Remember that it will fire one more shot even if you hit it, so don't stay where you are.

The second cannon will then begin moving lower and lower while you handle some attackers. If it moves too low for you to risk going under it, don't worry: it soon shifts back to the top of the screen.

g. Against the Galaxians, take advantage of the vertical mobility you do not possess in the original game. Stay low most of the time, but rise if an attacker is about to ram you from the side.

During the early rounds, when you have time, shoot the robots at the top of the screen. Use GALAXIAN tactics to destroy attackers; as the game progresses, you will have to spend more and more time at the bottom of the screen.

h. In Mission Four, never take your eyes off the black hole. You will know exactly when meteorites and aliens appear and where they are headed; also, you will know from the number of dots around the hole how many more you must shoot.

In early rounds, keep your ship as close to the black hole as you can, moving it only from side to side to dodge meteorites. Later on, the aliens will come out so quickly that you might want to retreat to the bottom to avoid being rammed whenever you miss one twice or more. As a rule, of course, your proximity, concentration, and reflexes will let you shoot each one almost as it emerges.

i. To shoot the flagship, begin by clearing away large chunks of the semicircular shell with rapid-fire. Then go for the ship itself, shooting end pieces off first and finishing them off before you hit the reactor. You should try to destroy the flagship before it comes down low enough to threaten you.

Take refuge in the top corners only in emergencies. After the first round, shoot the Gorfian robots on the ship as soon as possible to stop them from distracting and endangering you in their suicide missions.

j. As you move up in the ranks, your strategy should not change drastically. Be more cautious about taking time and chances for the sake of maximum points. Minimum score for 35 missions amounts to more than maximum score for 25; as you get promoted, the risks increase.

6. MOON CRESTA

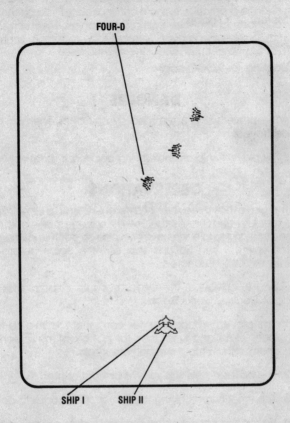

FOUR-D

SHIP I   SHIP II

CONTROLS

a. Left and right directional buttons

b. FIRE button

SCORING

a. Cold Eye: 50 points for each half

b. Super Fly: 30 points

c. Four-D: 60 points

d. Meteor: 200 points

e. Atomic Pile: 100 points

f. Docking: 0–9,000 points

DANGERS

a. If the player's ship is rammed by any of its enemies, it is destroyed.

b. If the player's ship crashes during docking, it is destroyed.

OBSERVATIONS

a. The player has three ships of different sizes: Ship I, small; Ship II, medium; and Ship III, large. The first has one missile port; the second and third each have two, one on each end. They all fire upward, and no one ship can fire again before its missiles have detonated.

b. During each round, the player has two opportunities to dock. Docking works like this:

   1. The player temporarily loses control of the ship he has been using, and it rises from the bottom of the screen to the middle without shifting horizontally.

   2. The next-smallest ship rises to bottom center.

   3. The timer begins, giving the player 30 seconds to dock.

   4. He regains control of the ship and tries to guide it to the center of the larger ship. It starts to fall either straight down or slightly to the left or right.

   5. He must use his left and right directional buttons to guide the ship; either will produce a descent at about a 45° angle.

   6. If the ship is too low to be able to shift it over far enough in time, the player can press the RETRO button to slow, halt, and even reverse its descent.

7. If one ship lands on the other too far from center, the top ship is vaporized and the next attack begins.

8. Once the ship manages to dock, the timer stops. The number of seconds remaining is multiplied by 100, 200, or 300: 100 if Ship I docked with Ship II or III; 200 if Ship II docked with Ship III; and 300 if Ships I and II, having docked together beforehand, docked with Ship III. The final product is what the player receives as a bonus.

The usual time remaining to a good player is 20 seconds, give or take 2. If a crash occurs or the time runs out, no bonus is received, and the player must continue without having docked.

c. After a successful docking, the player has much more firepower. If he has docked Ship I to Ship II, for example, he can have one, two, or three missiles in the air whenever he wants. Ship II, you see, can fire on either side of Ship I, just as Ship III, with its even greater width, can fire on either side of Ship II.

The separate ships still cannot fire until their missiles have detonated; for instance, if Ship I's missile has but Ship II's have not, only Ship I can then fire. Pressing FIRE again will prouduce no results until Ship II's missles both detonate.

When all three ships are together, the player can have an overwhelming five missiles in the air at once just by pressing FIRE three times quickly, once for each ship.

d. What happens when an enemy rams docked ships? Only one of the ships survives, either the top or the bottom one.

e. The first three types of attackers—Cold Eye, Super Fly, and Four-D—share certain flight patterns. Since none of them shoots, they must fly evasively to threaten the player's ship.

First of all, they all stay in the top two-thirds of the screen for about five seconds. When they do come down low enough to ram the player's ship, they execute a regular series of semicircles that can double back or combine to form buttonhooks and squiggles. The maneuvers soon become recognizable, even predictable.

After spending a few seconds in the bottom third of the screen, they exit at the bottom or side and rematerialize in their original positions. They are easy targets for about one second when they rematerialize.

f. As in GALAXIAN, the bottom corners of the screen are usually safe for the player's ship in emergencies.

g. The attacks come in the following sequence: two waves of Cold Eye, two waves of Super Fly, docking, two waves of Four-D, one wave of meteors, docking, two waves of Atomic Pile. When the player loses a ship, he must still finish off that wave to go on to the next.

h. Each wave of four Cold Eyes materializes in a horizontal diamond formation, with one on each end and two in the middle, one just above the other. Cold Eyes are roughly circular, with halves that can act independently. Hitting a Cold Eye leaves one half; if a Cold Eye is not hit, it stays together for about ten seconds and then splits anyway.

If the player begins to shoot right away from bottom center, he will hit the lowest Cold Eye as it materializes; if he continues shooting, he will have knocked off at least five halves out of eight by the time they descend to his level.

i. Each wave of eight Super Flies (the names are Nichibutsu's, not mine) materializes two at a time, each pair moving away to be replaced by the next. All eight appear on the screen within four seconds.

j. Each wave of Four-Ds materializes in two sets of four, two on each side of the screen. They are larger than Super Flies and, therefore, easier targets. As usual, the second wave does not appear until the first has been entirely eliminated.

k. The meteor attack consists of eight pairs. One meteor emerges from high on the left edge of the screen, and one from the right. The two streak in simultaneous diagonals, crossing paths near the bottom.

If the player keeps his ship in either of the bottom corners, the meteors will not touch it. Once the 16 meteors go by, the attack is over.

l. Next come the Atomic Piles, deadly blocks that always fall straight. They can fall alone or tipped by narrow rods, but they always start at the top of the screen. After a certain amount of time, the attack ceases, even if not all the enemies have been destroyed.

m. Later rounds are different from the first in only three instances:

   1. The Cold Eyes fly more evasively and aggressively.

   2. There is no docking if the player has only one ship left. If he has more than one, the process starts over, and the smallest remaining ship is the first to face attackers.

      This system of repetition is unfortunate in a way, since the player can kill the creatures more quickly with two or three ships than with one; on the other hand, if he does survive two attacks, he will earn a large bonus by docking and then possess greater firepower, anyway.

   3. In the first round, only one Atomic Pile can attack at a time; in the second round, two; and from the eighth round on, all eight descend at once, making safety without shooting impossible.

n. There is a new version of MOON CRESTA in which attackers can shoot as well as ram, the player's shots move much more quickly, and high scorers can sign with ten letters instead of the usual three.

STRATEGIES

a. Shoot constantly when you have one ship, as in most SPACE INVADERS-type games.

b. As you begin docking, let the ship fall on its own for a second to see where it's headed, then press a button only if you need to. The rule is to save time by using the controls as little as possible.

   Learn how far from center you can afford to be when the ships touch. If you're too far to the side, take the time to push RETRO and set matters right.

The least desirable outcome is a crash; if you seem about to crash, press all the way to the side, missing the bottom ship altogether. Your only loss will be the time it then takes to retro back up to docking position. Remember, the loss of any ship will affect your play the rest of the game.

c. After docking, use your new firepower judiciously. You should always have at least one missile near the middle of the screen.

If you have all three ships to fire with, pressing three times rapidly produces an appealing arrowhead effect, but this may not be the most efficient way. If you delay ever so slightly before pressing each time, your first shot will have detonated by the time your third is out, so you will be able to fire again right away, maintaining a constant stream of evenly-spaced missiles for as long as you want. That way, you can take care of all the enemies that fly over you rather than just most of them.

d. Once you have managed to assemble your triple ship, your firepower decreases your chances of destruction more than your size increases them. Take special care, though, not to get hit; if you are, you may lose two ships at a blow.

e. If you learn the enemy flight patterns, you will have little trouble in evading and eliminating attackers quickly.

f. Retreat to a bottom corner when an enemy is at your level and heading towards you. Never linger there, however.

Be especially wary of attackers that dip below your ship. They may come up right into you in a buttonhook maneuver. There is no threat, however, when an attacker is more than three inches to one side of you; they never make horizontal squiggles longer than that.

g. Spend the first ten seconds of a Cold Eye attack shooting quickly from bottom center; of a Super Fly attack, from an inch left of center; and of a Four-D attack, from an inch right of center.

Once seven seconds are up, be sure to dodge any survivors that wander down. When they finally exit, you know they will probably rematerialize where you **haven't** been shooting, so shift over to polish off the stragglers.

h. Sticking to one corner or the other to escape meteors is not excessive timidity as long as you try to shoot a few. Hitting more than one out of each pair is almost impossible because of their speed.

Between pairs, slip over about two inches and shoot as soon as the meteors appear. Whether you hit or not, you must retreat immediately. The one you fire at is heading toward the opposite side; the other is coming at you.

There is sometimes a safe spot at bottom center, when the two cross paths high enough. You can't tell in advance whether they will, though, so retreating to this spot is risky.

i. Shoot as many Atomic Piles as you can for maximum points. Dodging is more important for surviving the attack, but a high score is nothing to avoid.

j. Know the sequence of attacks. Being in the right place when each one starts can save your ship. Remember especially not to sit where you are after annihilating the second Four-D wave; if you do, chances are good you'll be mashed by a meteor.

Even in the other attacks, though, firing a second early in just the right place will give you a potentially valuable head start.

k. Increase caution as the game progresses. Against the Atomic Piles especially, you will need to shoot immediately. By the eighth round, you will need to hit one or two to survive their attack for a second.

l. If you encounter the new version of MOON CRESTA and want to learn it, you'll be making a good investment if you play regular MOON CRESTA or EAGLE, a similar game, first. You can thus learn the game's patterns without the pressure of being fired at constantly.

7. PHOENIX

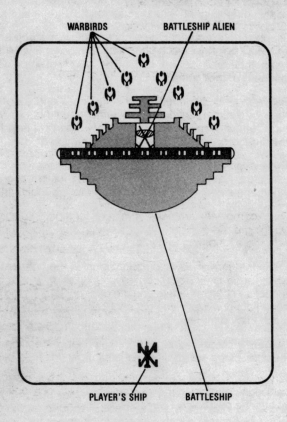

WARBIRDS   BATTLESHIP ALIEN

PLAYER'S SHIP   BATTLESHIP

CONTROLS

a. Left and right directional buttons

b. FIRE button

c. SHIELD button

SCORING

a. 20, 40, or 200 points for each warbird

b. 50 points for each phoenix egg

c. 20 points for each phoenix wing

d. 100-900 points for each phoenix

e. 400 or more points for each battleship alien

f. Bonus ship at 5,000 points

DANGERS

a. Collision with warbirds, phoenixes, the battleship, or any of their bombs destroys the player's ship.

OBSERVATIONS

a. The player's ship can have only one missile in the air at a time except during the second warbird attack in each round, when it can have two. The player's missiles have no effect on enemy bombs.

b. Pressing SHIELD surrounds the ship with a force field that destroys any bombs or birds that touch it. It lasts about three seconds, during which the ship can shoot but not move. Afterwards, the shield cannot be used for approximately five seconds unless the ship is destroyed or the attack is completed.

c. Every warbird makes sounds to indicate how it is flying. The cacophony of many birds is useless, but, with only one or two left, the sounds can be useful for strategy.

Phoenixes cry out only when hit, and the player's ship produces sounds whenever it fires or is destroyed.

d. Each round consists of five attacks: two warbird attacks, two phoenix attacks, and a battleship attack. If the player's ship is destroyed in the middle of an attack, the surviving birds confront its replacement in a new formation.

e. The warbirds in the first two attacks appear in symmetrical formations from which they fall a few at a time to beleaguer the player. The surviving warbirds return to their original places, where they use their little wings to walk from side to side.

Attackers employ several aggressive flight patterns, dropping bombs only when they are directly over the player's ship. They flutter in circles or semicircles, periodically returning to upright positions and taking a few lateral steps before fluttering off again. They are dangerous when they walk on the same level as the ship or even slightly below; when they start flying again, they sometimes ram it from beneath.

Warbirds are worth 20 points when upright, 40 when attacking, and 200 when ascending with wings outspread. Amstar, which licensed Centuri to manufacture PHOENIX, claims that a warbird can also be worth 80 points, but I have yet seen or heard of such a score.

f. Similarly, Amstar neglects to mention that a wing hit on a phoenix is worth 20 points. Each wave of phoenixes starts out as eight colorful eggs in the top half of the screen, which fly without firing for about six seconds. They then change gradually into menacing phoenixes, larger and quicker than the warbirds.

The eggs are 50 points each, but the full-grown birds can yield randomly any multiple of 10 from 100 to 900 (never much more than 500 points in the first several rounds). Wing hits do not disable phoenixes; they still swoop from side to side, descending slightly with each crossing. One thing to notice is that they always slow down slightly at the edges.

g. The battleship is defended in the first round by a formation of warbirds above it that fly independently of it just as in their own attacks, although they are shielded from the player's fire when in formation. When the last warbird of the group is shot, the entire group is replaced.

The battleship, meanwhile, descends slowly, along with the alien it carries. The lower the battleship, the more its passenger is worth. The alien is protected by the thick orange underside of the battleship and by a revolving purple belt, both of which must be shot through before it can perish. The belt itself is exposed at the battleship's left and right extremities.

h. From the second round on, the battleship has an extra line of warbird escorts riding just above the purple belt. Other differences in later rounds are that the first two attacks begin with different formations and that the phoenixes sometimes start with mass kamikaze attacks, after which they are just as easy as in the first round.

STRATEGIES

a. Shoot whenever you have a target. Shooting bombs won't help, so dodge when you must.

b. Do not press SHIELD until just before you have to, since it might wear out before it should. It can be a weapon, too, of course; if a warbird is upright at or below your level, shift over to it and then zap it with the force field.

c. Ignore the sound effects until only one or two warbirds remain; then listen as an aid to keeping pace with their maneuvers.

d. Know the sequence of attacks. It pays to be where you need to be as soon as you can.

e. Move with the warbirds when you want to kill them in formation. Most of the time, though, you should try for maximum points by hitting them when they are flapping or at least attacking. Since they aim their bombs at you, you should always be on the move.

f. Phoenixes are most vulnerable at the sides of the screen. After hitting a few eggs, hurry to the left or right bottom corner and keep shooting. All you need to look out for are rare bombs from above, which you can easily dodge, and ramming attempts from the side, which you can thwart with your shield.

g. Don't shoot all the battleship's warbirds unless you want to deal with a new group. I believe in shooting away the purple belt first where it is exposed on the left or right. Since it is always moving, you must make many holes in it, meanwhile eliminating any warbirds that come too close. The whole procedure should take only about 15 seconds.

Then slide to center and bore through the hull of the battleship with rapid-fire. If you are confident enough, you can wait until the battleship comes very low before finishing off the alien.

h. Know how the game gets more difficult; thus, you will be ready for sudden kamikaze attacks. The action moves slowly enough so that you never have to suffer unpleasant surprises.

8. PLEIADES

RADAR DISHES   EARTH STATION   AIRSTRIP TARGET

FLAG   PLAYER'S SHIP   UNMANNED SHIPS

CONTROLS

a. Left and right directional buttons

b. FIRE button

c. WARP button

SCORING

a. No. 1 Martian: 30 points

b. No. 2 Martian: 80 points

c. Martian UFO: 150 points

d. Space monster: 20, 50, 100, 200, or 400 points

e. Battleship: 0-9,600 points

f. Airstrip flag: 100-600 points

g. Airstrip target: 500-4,000 points

h. Bonus for finishing each fleet of Martians

i. Extra ship at 5,000 points

DANGERS

a. Martians try to bomb or ram ship.

b. Space monsters try to bomb or ram ship.

c. If the ship crashes on the airstrip, it is destroyed.

OBSERVATIONS

a. The player's ship can have any number of shots on the screen at a time and can move along the bottom more quickly than in most SPACE INVADERS-type games, so its overall capabilities are considerable.

b. Warp fulfills a hyperspace function, instantly transporting the player's ship to a randomly chosen spot along the bottom. It does not have unlimited use but is very rarely, if ever, necessary for a good player.

c. The game has rounds composed of four very different sectors. The specifics below show how each Sector Four always leads into the next Sector One.

d. Sector One–Earth's atmosphere is the battleground. The player's ship must protect various fuel tanks, unmanned ships, and radar dishes in the bottom corners against hostile Martians.

No. 1 Martians come in waves of three in the first round; whichever ones survive long enough either go off the side of the screen to return as dangerous UFOs or gradually change into No. 2 Martians, which descend to station level and lay down bricks, shooting all the while. The bricks let enemy shots through but must be shot away by the player to clear his own line of fire.

All the other objects at Earth Station protect the player until they are shot away, serving as friendly counterparts to the Martians' bricks. The radar dishes, in fact, do even more. They often nod between waves to indicate where the next one will appear. They fire bullets that sometimes destroy Martians, and the player receives the credit. Thus, it is worse to lose a radar dish than to lose a fuel tank.

The last Martian to die yields a higher score than the others: its regular value plus the round number multiplied by 100. If, for instance, during his fourth time at Earth Station, the player kills a No. 1 Martian last, he scores 430 points. Two fleets of Martians appear each round, producing two bonus scores: one in Sector One and one in Sector Three (see Observation f).

e. Sector Two: The player must face eight space monsters. Here are some observations about their behavior:

1. They start small and high in the screen; a shot anywhere will kill them as they flit across and down.

2. After five seconds, they begin to grow, develop teeth and eyes, and start to drop bombs from their midsections. They also swoop down more and more quickly as the seconds pass, reappearing at the top each time. The three missiles they release while crossing the screen are particularly dangerous, since they can be spread out over two inches and, thus, harder to dodge.

3. A center hit destroys the monster, but a wing hit disables it so that it can fly only straight down. Unfortunately, it recuperates from the wound within seconds.

4. The monsters are 50 points each before reaching full size. Once they do, a wing hit is 20, while a center hit is

100, 200, or 400, depending on whether the monster has no wing wounds, one wing wound, or two wing wounds.

f. Sector Three: The Martian battleship is at the top of the screen. The player's goal is to destroy it in one of two ways: either by killing all the Martians that emerge from the ship and the edge, or by destroying all five of the ship's engines.

1. The Martians are identical to those in Sector One, except that there are no Martians of the No. 2 variety. The ones from the battleship emerge several at a time through portholes.

2. There are five portholes, one above each engine. They open and close one at a time in random order, releasing Martians either straight down or diagonally.

3. Martians flying above the battleship cannot be hit by shots from below.

4. To destroy an engine, the player must shoot it when the porthole above it is open. Shots fired at any other time have no effect. The last engines are harder to destroy than the first, since one porthole often opens twice before others open even once, making the player wait for a chance to shoot. Also, Martian attacks grow more deadly when they are not dealt with immediately.

5. A word on scoring: the battleship's value registers in red numerals directly above it. It starts at 0 every round, but when the first engine is hit, it rises to the round number multiplied by 100, through the sixth round. Every engine destroyed thereafter doubles the battleship's value; thus, it can rise to as high as 9,600 from the sixth round on.

g. Sector Four: Here the player must taxi along a runway, weaving among other ships to reach the target at the end. Only the directional buttons are used. The ships are stationary, but the player moves up along the runway at a constant rate, and he must be careful to avoid them.

Two or three flags appear randomly among the ships. If the

player can touch one, it disappears and yields a random value of from 100 to 600 points.

The player's ship rotates along a lengthwise axis, with the effect of growing narrower and broader as it moves to the right or left. It is responding to an SOS from its home planet; in fact, Earth Station appears just beyond the airstrip, with the radar dishes waving once in greeting.

The target at the end gives from 500 to 4,000 points, depending on accuracy. If the player has an accident there or anywhere else on the runway, he scores no points and must start over at the base of the airstrip.

h. The action moves somewhat more quickly in later rounds, but what makes them more difficult is that the Martian fleets in Sectors One and Three attack in larger waves each time. Instead of coming three at a time, they eventually attack in groups of six or more.

STRATEGIES

a. Use WARP only in emergencies, unless you want to risk materializing under a space monster or Martian.

b. Shoot as quickly as possible. The more you fire, the more missiles will head toward your enemies.

c. In Sector One, kill your attackers off quickly. Use the radar dishes for forewarning and extra firepower, and don't let them get knocked out if you can help it.

Shoot your enemies' bricks away to clear your line of fire, but be very careful of the No. 2 Martians, since they shoot once with each brick they lay down.

When a UFO infiltrates the station, it wants to ram you. Move away.

d. You will notice that the space monsters fly in definite patterns during their 50-point stage. In the first round, for instance, firing steadily from bottom left should eliminate almost all of them before they can grow.

Once they do, of course, you want as few of them swooping down on you as possible. You must wound the survivors immediately to make them less of a threat, and don't give them time to recuperate.

The monsters are worth more full-sized, so let as many grow as you think you can handle. Here's a trick for extra points when only one is left: wound it and keep shooting one wing, forcing the monster to travel straight down the screen over and over. Dodge whenever it nears the bottom, of course, and slip back into position as soon as it passes.

It eventually moves too quickly to exploit in this manner, so you must kill it before it crushes you or its wounds heal. Hitting both wings before the center will give you 400 points; in the meantime, 20 points for every wing hit could earn you well over 1,000.

e. Shoot as many of the battleship's engines as you can. If you must dodge Martians to prolong the sector and to hit all the engines, remember that the Martians you don't shoot come back more deadly than before.

Watch the portholes and shoot the instant one opens. Otherwise you may be too beset by attackers to fire at the engine before the porthole closes. If there are too many Martians around you to dodge, you have no choice but to shoot them even if it means ending the sector prematurely.

f. In Sector Four, pushing either directional button too hard or for too long may give you unwanted lateral velocity. It is better to tap them alternately, keeping firm control of the ship.

Try for the flags only when touching them does not involve undue risk. Once you reach the end of the airstrip, steer the tip of your ship as close to target center as possible.

g. As the game progresses, you will have to shoot more and more quickly and accurately.

9. SPACE INVADERS

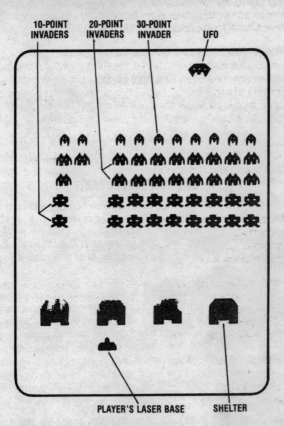

10-POINT
INVADERS

20-POINT
INVADERS

30-POINT
INVADER

UFO

PLAYER'S LASER BASE   SHELTER

CONTROLS

a. Left and right directional buttons

b. FIRE button

SCORING

a. 10 points for any invader in the bottom two rows

b. 20 points for any invader in the next two rows

c. 30 points for any invader in the top row

d. 50, 100, 150, or 300 points for each UFO

e. Bonus laser base at 1,000 points

DANGERS

a. When the laser base is hit by an enemy missile, it is destroyed.

b. When the player loses all his laser bases or permits any number of invaders to reach the bottom row, the game ends.

OBSERVATIONS

a. The player's laser bases materialize at bottom left and can have only one shot on the screen at a time.

b. The four shelters protect the player until they are gradually destroyed by the invaders' missiles and the player's own laser.

c. The invaders are arranged in five rows of 11. They always move sideways until they hit one edge of the screen, when they all drop one level and start to move toward the opposite side. The different rows do not always move at the same rate, so that one invader may protrude slightly over the one beneath it.

In the first screen the invaders need to drop only 11 levels to reach the bottom of the screen and end the game.

d. The more invaders in a screen the player shoots, the faster the survivors move. When only eight are left, their speed increases dramatically. When they come low enough, the invaders destroy the shelters by erasing whatever parts they pass through, but the player receives new shelters with each screen.

e. The last invader in each screen moves very fast, but slightly more slowly from right to left than from left to right.

f. No invader can fire missiles when it is in the second row from the bottom, known as "death row."

g. No one invader can ever have more than three missiles on the screen at a time. Missiles are fired randomly from the center of each invader and come in three recognizable varieties: slow straight ones, fast straight ones, and squiggly ones that do the most damage.

h. When a missile and a laser shot collide, both usually detonate, although the missile sometimes continues to descend. The laser shot never survives.

i. UFOs travel across the top of the screen at an unchanging velocity every 25 seconds, appearing at top left and top right in equal proportion. Once fewer than 9 out of 55 invaders remain, the UFOs cease until the next screen.

Careful experimentation has proven that their values are not determined by any REG, but depend on the number of shots the player takes between UFOs. They are worth 300 points only when hit on the twenty-third shot of each screen or every fifteenth shot thereafter.

j. The second screen of invaders starts one level lower than the first. The invaders begin yet another level lower in the third screen, another in the fourth, and another in the seventh, although they regain their original height in the tenth, which is understandably difficult to reach.

STRATEGIES

a. Start shooting and maneuvering the instant your laser base appears on the screen, and don't stop from then on.

b. Beware of shelters that have sustained damage. They are not always entirely safe to stay under.

c. You can use shelters when shooting, however, in either of two ways:

   1. Stay half under the shelter with your nozzle just far enough to the side to shoot.

   2. If the center of the shelter is already damaged, shoot a clear hole through it and fire at the invaders from there.

Both these strategic positions are best for shooting invaders column by column. Some players, however, prefer to annihilate the first few screens row by row or in no order at all.

d. You must learn to kill the invaders as quickly as possible while still evading their missiles. Develop a move-shoot-dodge rhythm for this purpose. Also try to shoot at the left or right section of each invader; thus your shot will rarely be wasted by a collision with a missile from your enemy's center. When a collision does occur, though, keep in mind that the missile may not be destroyed.

e. In the course of each screen, adjust your timing to your adversaries' gradually increasing speed.

f. Once you have the 55 whittled down to 1, don't forget that the lone survivor moves very quickly and is constantly firing missiles. It is usually easier to shoot as it travels from right to left; you should remain in one place for maximum accuracy. curacy.

g. Take the trouble to count your shots; high UFO scores can double or triple your final score. It is possible, in fact, for a skillful player to shoot eight 300-point UFOs during the first screen, six during the second, and four during the third. Not bad, considering that a whole screen of invaders totals only 990 points.

h. During the first three rounds, the only strategy you need is to shoot the columns of invaders on the ends, making the formation descend more slowly. You want each screen to last as long as possible to give the maximum number of UFOs a chance to appear. From the fourth screen on, however, the invaders will start so low that eliminating them becomes more urgent than getting high UFO scores.

i. For these more difficult screens, experts have devised this effective technique:

1. Begin the screen normally by shooting all the invaders but the four or five columns on the right and a 30-pointer two or three columns to the left of them. The space between the large block and the single invader will be your safe spot for the rest of the game.

2. Stay there, shifting with the invaders when you must, and hunt 300-point UFOs until the bottom row of invaders has reached death row. You know they cannot shoot, so slip under them to the right without firing. Then return to your original safe spot, stopping to pick the bottom row off one by one before they drop down.

3. Repeat this process as soon as the next row descends, and keep doing it until only the five or six 30-pointers are left. You can slide under the ones to your right and then shoot all five or six as they whiz past, ending the screen.

4. You see why you can keep only four or five columns on the right: any more would be too many to risk hitting one by one five times, and any fewer would make the last two rows accelerate suddenly. This way, you have at least nine invaders left when you begin to demolish the second-to-last row.

5. The only disadvantage to the system is that one miss ends the game, but the difficulty of later screens leaves you with little choice. You will survive if you can develop a simple move-stop-shoot rhythm to the left that can accelerate along with the invaders.

10. SPACE INVADERS PART II

30-POINT INVADER   20-POINT INVADERS

SHELTERS   PLAYER'S   10-POINT
            LASER BASE   INVADERS

CONTROLS

a. Left and right directional buttons

b. FIRE button

SCORING

The same as in SPACE INVADERS with two additions:

a. 30 points for each twin invader

60

b. 200 or 500 points for each flashing UFO, depending on the manufacturer

DANGERS

The same as in SPACE INVADERS

OBSERVATIONS

Everything is the same as in SPACE INVADERS with the following exceptions:

a. The background is no longer plain black, but a drawing of a futuristic Terran city. In addition, the shelters all show the screen number.

b. The scoreboard can accommodate 99,990 points, as opposed to a mere 9,990; in addition, high scorers can sign with ten letters instead of three.

c. If the player manages to shoot the top four invaders in the column on the left before he shoots the bottom one, he earns 1,000 points. If he achieves the same with any other column, he earns 500.

Taito, which manufactures the game and has also licensed it to Midway, promises a wonderful rainbow explosion when any player manages to shoot a 10-point invader last out of all 55, but I have yet to see that feat accomplished.

d. One UFO flashes during each screen, traveling across the screen at a normal pace but vulnerable only when it is visible. It is always worth 200 points in Midway's model and 500 in Taito's.

e. From the second screen on in Midway's version and the fourth screen on in Taito's version, only 52 invaders appear in each screen. The catch is that when hit, many of these 52 divide into small twins, which immediately commence moving and firing.

They are difficult targets because of their size and their ability to grow and shrink in time with the heartbeat of the machine. It should be noted, however, that two splitting invaders, when hit next to each other, yield not four but three small replacements.

f. From the third screen on, the flashing UFO often drops rein-forcements randomly into the top row of invaders. The pro-grammers of SPACE INVADERS PART II are quite innovative.

STRATEGIES

a. All the SPACE INVADERS strategies work just as well for the new game, including the technique for later screens.

All you have to do is shoot the splitting invaders two at a time to fill in the holes in their row of five before you slide under it near the end. The only other precaution necessary is to prevent the flashing UFO's reinforcements from jeopar-dizing your safe spot.

b. Try for the new bonuses if you feel you can spare the time; otherwise, don't bother. The first screen is the best time to attempt them.

5
ASTEROIDS-TYPE GAMES

11. ASTEROIDS

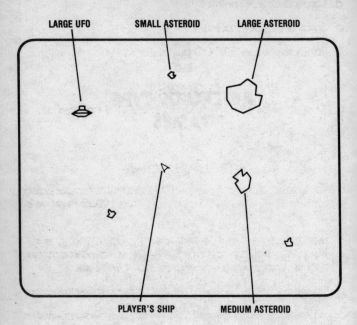

LARGE UFO   SMALL ASTEROID   LARGE ASTEROID

PLAYER'S SHIP   MEDIUM ASTEROID

CONTROLS

a. ROTATE buttons, one to the left and one to the right.

b. THRUST button

c. FIRE button

d. HYPERSPACE button

SCORING

a. Large asteroid: 20 points

b. Medium asteroid: 50 points

c. Small asteroid: 100 points

d. Large UFO: 200 points

e. Small UFO: 1,000 points

f. Bonus ship every 10,000 points

DANGERS

a. If ship collides with any asteroid or UFO, it is destroyed.

b. UFOs fire at ship.

OBSERVATIONS

a. The ship's steering is more sophisticated than in most video games. It is possible to go straight, to stand still, or to move in a curve.

Many beginners take some time to realize that it is impossible to thrust in one direction while shooting in another, and so have trouble covering their own retreats.

b. The player can have up to four shots on the screen at once.

c. Hyperspace is risky, since the player's ship may rematerialize in a fatal location.

d. If the player's score is 99,990, the next points will "turn the machine over," or return the score to 0.

e. The first screen begins with 4 large asteroids; that number increases from screen to screen but never exceeds 16.

_ The asteroids always start at the edges of the screen and float toward the center. A shot will split a large asteroid into two medium ones and a medium asteroid into two small ones.

f. Depending on the angle from which an asteroid is hit, its two fragments may pick up speed or slow down; thus small asteroids have the greatest potential for speed and, because of their size, are also the hardest to see and to shoot. At least the player knows that a small asteroid will disappear and not divide when he shoots it.

g. When a ship is destroyed before the end of a screen, action does not stop while its replacement appears at center. The machine is programmed to wait until there are no asteroids within about an inch of the spot; then the new ship appears at exactly the same angle its predecessor held at death.

h. The large UFOs shoot at random, but the small ones zero in on the ship. Neither one, however, can shoot over the edge of the screen. In other words, the shots cannot disappear off one edge and reappear from the opposite one; the player's shots can.

UFOs come from the sides of the screen–never the top or bottom edges–and wait at least three-quarters of a second before they begin firing.

i. The asteroids pass through one another without incident, but a UFO crashes into them just as the player's ship does, except that the crash produces no points. Occasionally, the trajectory of an asteroid is altered by a UFO collision in such a way that the player's ship is suddenly endangered.

STRATEGIES

a. Half the technique of the game lies in the handling of the ship, so learn to do it well. Learn also to predict how each asteroid you shoot at will break, and try if you can to slow it down with your shot.

b. Use the edges to your advantage. You must know exactly where and in what direction your ship or your shot will emerge onto the screen. Automatic awareness of your future whereabouts will net you many points.

c. Stay away from edges whenever there are more asteroids than you can keep track of; otherwise, you run the risk of unexpected collision.

d. It is a good idea not to move too much at the beginning of a screen, since it is easier to aim when you are rotating without thrust. Some players hit only one or two large asteroids at a time and destroy all the fragments before continuing, but confidence in your maneuvering ability should let you blast away until the screen is almost cleared.

e. Shoot in frequent bursts of two when you start a screen. Two is the right number: one would be too few to guarantee destruction and, if you shoot three or even four in one burst, you might be unable to fire at all if an emergency ensues. Reserve shots never hurt.

The closer you are to your target, the sooner you can refire once it is hit. Evade asteroids approaching within an inch of you, though; if you fire, a fragment may demolish you. If a large asteroid is close but moving away, you can fire a burst of four, secure in the knowledge that at least two shots will immediately find their marks.

f. Be careful whenever you have just had a ship destroyed; your next may materialize in a bad position at the center.

g. Good players usually do without hyperspace, even in emergencies.

h. When you are threatened by a small UFO, flying around it is the best way to prevent its getting a bead on you. Shooting at the same time is tricky, but you can pinpoint your target by using your peripheral vision and knowing the direction from which the target's shots are coming.

i. If you are out to get points, you can use the infamous method of "hunting":

    1. Eliminate the entire screen except for one small or medium asteroid.

    2. Ambush UFOs as they appear.

If hunting strikes you as the wrong way to play, either don't use it or play ASTEROIDS DELUXE, in which it is impossible.

j. An expert hunter can make one game of ASTEROIDS go a long way–in fact, over fifty hours! You must be careful to protect your single asteroid; if a UFO does happen to destroy it, move to the center before the next screen appears.

k. "Ambush UFOs as they appear," says Strategy i. Easier said than done? Not once you have the knack of it. There are actually two different methods, one more popular than the other. Here are both:

1. Being careful to avoid the asteroid, thrust your ship up along the center of the screen over and over; when you turn to fire at UFOs the instant they appear, your upward momentum will keep you moving in a vertical line, and even the small ones will not be able to track you.

2. Wayne McLemore, a current high scorer, stations his ship in the upper left or right corner about an inch from the side. When a UFO emerges from his side of the screen, he picks it off before it can even fire; when it emerges from the opposite side, he shoots behind the screen with almost equal accuracy. Knowing the proper angles takes some practice, but the results are well worth it.

I. If you are interested in trying to break the record, this is how it's done: The machine gives a bonus ship with **every** 10,000 points, so it is possible to acccumulate over a hundred of them. When you need to take time out, all you do is sacrifice a small percentage of your stock of ships. Theoretically, the game can go on forever that way.

12. ASTEROIDS DELUXE

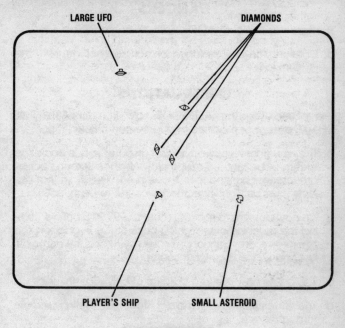

LARGE UFO   DIAMONDS

PLAYER'S SHIP   SMALL ASTEROID

CONTROLS

a. Left and right ROTATE buttons

b. THRUST button

c. FIRE button

d. SHIELD button

SCORING

Identical to that of ASTEROIDS except for three additions:

a. Hexagon: 50 points

b. Diamond: 100 points

c. Wedge: 200 points

DANGERS

The same as those for ASTEROIDS with one addition:

a. Collision with any hexagon or part thereof destroys the player's ship.

OBSERVATIONS

The observations for ASTEROIDS hold true for ASTEROIDS DELUXE except as modified or augmented below:

a. The new game is played against an outer-space backdrop that must be ignored during play. Also, the screen's edges are less well defined than those in ASTEROIDS, so that objects must be slightly nearer the center to be in focus.

b. It is now possible to reach a score of 999,990 before "turning the machine over" (going back to 0). In addition, the top three scores cannot be erased by turning the game off, but only by getting higher scores.

c. The game now allows a build-up of only 10 extra ships.

d. The asteroids now tumble instead of drifting straight through space.

e. The first screen contains six large asteroids, as opposed to four in the original game. On the brighter side, no screen begins with more than 9 large asteroids, whereas the original game could go up to 16. The reason for this limited scope is that the new game's circuits are too busy with UFO accuracy, asteroid rotation, and hexagons to handle more than nine large rocks.

f. The large UFO now shoots with deadly accuracy. Three out of every four shots are directed at asteroids; the fourth, at the player's ship.

g. The small UFO, for its part, is more lethal than ever. It shoots at asteroids only once for every two shots it takes at the player's ship. Both UFOs appear in the same manner they do in ASTEROIDS.

h. Each hexagonal cluster drifts until it is hit; it then splits into three diamonds, which try to ram the player's ship. Each diamond, when hit, splits in turn into two wedges, which rotate until they point to the player's ship and make an even quicker beeline for it until they reach it or are destroyed.

i. The shield protects the player's ship from any attack except a double ram: it is possible for even a shielded ship to be crushed between two asteroids, two wedges, or an asteroid and a wedge.

   A shielded ship cannot shoot, but it can rotate and thrust. When its shield hits a UFO, large or small, the enemy ship is destroyed. Unfortunately, the shield runs out after only a few seconds' use and can give way at any moment until it is recharged with the beginning of a new screen.

j. In later screens, everything speeds up as it does in ASTEROIDS, and the wedges become fast enough to outrun a ship. After the player has used 30 ships, though, everything returns to its original level of difficulty.

k. ASTEROIDS DELUXE is a difficult game: the current world record is only 269,230 points in an hour and seven minutes. Operators are concerned that few people will want to face such a challenge once the novelty wears off, so they have released an optional new circuit which makes the game easier in the following ways:

   1. The UFOs shoot somewhat more randomly.

   2. The first round starts with four large asteroids instead of six.

After 30,000 points, though, there is no appreciable difference between the two programs.

STRATEGIES

a. Stay clear of the edges as much as possible, because you may not see an asteroid or a UFO until it's too late.

b. Because the UFOs shoot asteroids deliberately now, hunting is no longer effective, and technique and handling are all the more important.

c. Be prepared for a UFO to hit an asteroid or, even worse, a hexagon near you, giving you two immediate dangers at once.

d. Save hexagons for the end of each screen, and escape from them by maneuvering until you shoot the last wedge.

e. Use your shield only in an emergency or when you are within ramming distance of a UFO.

f. From the first screen, find out whether the machine you are playing has the new circuit or not (see Observation k). The knowledge could be useful.

13. DEFENDER

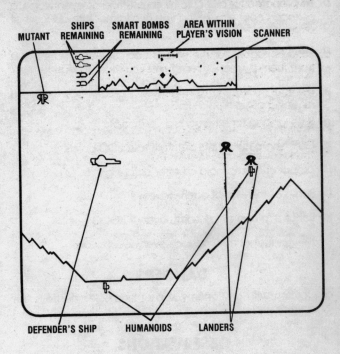

MUTANT   SHIPS REMAINING   SMART BOMBS REMAINING   AREA WITHIN PLAYER'S VISION   SCANNER

DEFENDER'S SHIP   HUMANOIDS   LANDERS

CONTROLS

a. Up-down lever

b. REVERSE button

c. THRUST button

d. FIRE button

e. SMART BOMB button

f. HYPERSPACE button

SCORING

a. Lander: 150 points

73

b. Mutant: 150 points

c. Baiter: 200 points

d. Bomber: 250 points

e. Pod: 1,000 points

f. Swarmer: 150 points

g. Safe landing for a humanoid: 250 points

h. Catching a humanoid before it falls: 500 points

i. Dropping a humanoid off after catching it: 500 points

j. Bonus at the end of each wave

k. Bonus ship and smart bomb every 10,000 points

l. New planet and humanoids every fourth wave.

DANGERS

a. Collision with any enemy ship or its missiles destroys the player's ship.

OBSERVATIONS

a. The screen is a representation of a planet's surface and atmosphere. The defender can travel anywhere, even under the planet's surface. As he flies, the terrain that he must protect moves past him.

b. Above the large picture is the scanner that shows what is happening far to either side of the action on the screen. Each member of the large cast of characters has its own distinctive mark on the scanner, so the player can always be conscious of where he is needed most.

c. The player's ship responds very quickly to the controls except that it occasionally builds up some momentum from heavy thrust. It can fire as often as the player wants it to in whatever direction it is facing, but the shots go no farther than the borders of the screen.

d. The player starts the game with 12 humanoids; his main goal is to protect them. When the last humanoid dies, the planet disappears, and the defender is alone in space against the bad guys—an undesirable situation. Humanoids can die by being shot, by being dropped from heights of more than an inch, or by being mutated.

They scream to the defender for help; the defender must respond by destroying the abductors—without destroying the humanoids—and deposit the humanoids safely back on the surface. He passes through them safely while they are in the ground, but he may accidentally shoot them when they are in the air or destroy himself and them by a collision when they are in the clutches of the dreaded landers.

At the end of each wave of landers, the player receives the following point bonus: the number of humanoids still living multiplied by the wave number multiplied by 100.

e. Landers appear in the atmosphere and fall to the planet, where they capture humanoids and begin to ascend with them. Like mutants, they fire white bombs at the player's ship.

f. The instant a lander and its captive reach the top of the screen, they merge to form a dangerous mutant. The humanoid is lost from then on. The only thing to do with a mutant is to kill it; the sooner, the better, since it tracks the player's ship, tracing its longitudinal position until it can charge from directly above or below.

g. Baiters are even more deadly. They appear when the player takes longer than necessary to finish a wave; first one appears, then two more, and so on. They are faster than a ship in full thrust; while they pursue, they fire white bombs and start a sloping crash course.

Like all the enemies but landers, baiters can exit at the bottom of the screen and emerge from the top or vice versa. It is impossible, of course, for any ship to exit at one side and emerge from the other.

h. Bombers move slowly but leave stationary white X's in their paths; these are lethal to the defender.

i.   When the player shoots a pod, it explodes into a cloud of red swarmers that immediately go for his ship. One pod appears in the second wave, and more and more appear later on.

j.   DEFENDER is unusual in that it gives the player unlimited use of hyperspace. The usual problem remains, though: he doesn't know where he'll wind up or in which direction he'll be facing.

k.   The player starts the game with three smart bombs. When he presses the button, one explodes, killing every enemy on the screen at that moment. Even the pods in front of the player's ship are completely destroyed; from those behind, though, a few swarmers may survive.

STRATEGIES

a.   You should descend below the planet's surface only when fleeing attackers; most of the time, you should be where the landers are.

b.   Use the scanner to determine where you go. It shows you not only where the most landers are, but even where there are humanoids being kidnapped.

c.   DEFENDER has very complicated controls, and you will never be more than a novice without mastering them, learning to use them as automatically as you breathe.

The single most important piece of advice concerning steering is this: don't thrust too much. If you do, you will either miss and have to turn back, or run into an enemy. The more you thrust, the further from the edge of the screen you move, and the less time you have to react to what you encounter on the way.

d.   When you are thrusting, move up and down and fire as quickly as you can. You will thus destroy many of your enemies almost as soon as they come on the screen, especially since the scanner will forewarn you. It is often a good policy to annihilate everything in your section of the atmosphere before you move on.

e. The only exception to this rule is when you have humanoids in trouble. Then your first concern must be to rush to the scene of the crime, trying to prevent it if possible. If you do shoot the kidnapper, **don't** shoot the humanoid or let it fall to its death. Apart from your needing it alive so you can keep your planet, catching it and dropping it off will take only two seconds but will earn you 1,000 points.

f. When eliminating landers and mutants, you must be careful to avoid their bombs, which you sometimes need to look for to see. Killing a mutant takes only a second; simply thrust, then reverse and adjust your height simultaneously, and shoot.

g. Baiters won't bother you much once you've learned the game; but in the meantime, you should know how to deal with them. Once one is chasing you, you must quickly reverse twice. The baiter will be confused and disoriented, giving you almost a second to blast it.

If, through some misfortune, there should be three or more baiters after you at once, you will probably have to use a smart bomb. If you manage to escape without one, do everything you can to complete the wave before they find you again.

h. Shoot bombers on sight, but look out for their little white X's.

i. The better you get, the more you should try to conserve your smart bombs; you will need them in later rounds. If you are an intermediate and can spare smart bombs, though, you can use them to exterminate swarmers. You must be careful to shoot the pod from far away, not giving any swarmers time to reach you before the smart bomb explodes.

If you want to escape swarmers without a smart bomb, you just have to keep reversing, thrusting, and shooting until they are all gone. It can be time-consuming when you're new at it.

j. As a rule, you should use smart bombs only in the most dire emergencies or for big points in later rounds. "Big points" means enough for a new smart bomb, because of all the pods on the screen. Watch out for stray swarmers, though.

k. Good players use hyperspace only when they have to, which means rarely. One possible scenario: you have lost your planet in the middle of the fourth wave and must bring your ship through the wave to get a new planet and new humanoids. So you keep dodging very carefully with hyperspace until there are more enemies on the screen than you can count. Then you wipe them all out with a smart bomb. What a feeling!

If you don't want to lose your planet at all, you might consider carrying a humanoid around with you throughout the fourth wave. As long as you and he are safe, you keep the planet. Remember, he hops off the instant you brush against the ground.

Mastering DEFENDER requires some perserverance, but most players find the effort worthwhile.

14. SCRAMBLE

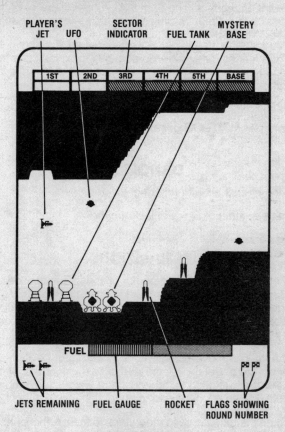

PLAYER'S JET   UFO   SECTOR INDICATOR   FUEL TANK   MYSTERY BASE

1ST   2ND   3RD   4TH   5TH   BASE

FUEL

JETS REMAINING   FUEL GAUGE   ROCKET   FLAGS SHOWING ROUND NUMBER

CONTROLS

a. Four-directional joystick

b. LASER button

c. BOMB button

SCORING

a. Rocket: 50 points on the ground, 80 points in the air

b. UFO: 100 points

c. Fuel tank: 150 points

d. Mystery base: 100, 200, or 300 points

e. Base: 800 points

f. 10 points every second

g. Bonus jet at 10,000 points

DANGERS

a. If the jet collides with anything, it is destroyed.

b. If the jet runs out of fuel, it is destroyed.

OBSERVATIONS

a. The jet can have only two bombs on the screen at once but can fire lasers in bursts of four that need not detonate or vanish before the next burst can be fired. Bombs fall in a diagonal trajectory, and lasers fire straight ahead to the right.

b. The jet can move up, down, or forward, but never back. When the player moves the joystick to the right, the jet accelerates in relation to the landscape, which always moves from right to left at a uniform pace.

When the player moves the joystick to the left, the jet stops in relation to the landscape until the movement of the landscape brings it against the left edge of the screen, forcing it forward in relation to the landscape.

Even when the joystick is all the way to the right or left, the jet can maneuver vertically.

c. Whenever a jet is destroyed, the next one appears with a new fuel supply at the beginning of the same sector. Fuel consumption is a function of time, independent of the jet's speed.

d. Fuel tanks, when hit, give the player both points and fuel. The values of mystery bases are determined randomly.

e. The player must pass through five sectors to reach the base. The sectors increase in difficulty and come in the same order every round.

f. Sector One presents little challenge. The jet flies over a hilly terrain littered with rockets, fuel tanks, and mystery bases. Every plateau, wide or narrow, has as many objects as can fit. The only real danger to the jet is that the rockets take off perpendicular to the planet whenever they reach the middle of the bottom edge, moving sideways with the rest of the landscape. If the player does not react in time; his jet is doomed.

g. In Sector Two, the only difference is the swarm of flitting UFOs that block the jet's path, a maximum of three or four on the screen at a time. They do not shoot and can be destroyed by laser or bombs, but collision with them is death.

h. In Sector Three, steering is more important than firing. Hordes of indestructible fireballs hurtle from right to left across the screen, traveling fast enough to make dodging them extremely risky even for the best players. The low hills at bottom, however, provide cover for the jet. The trick is to destroy the fuel tanks and mystery bases in the valleys and to dart from valley to valley without hitting the fireballs that zoom every now and then just over the hilltops.

i. Once the player makes it through the fireballs, he enters a series of tall buildings of varying heights over which he must fly in a relatively narrow airspace. Targets of all kinds perch on rooftops, and rockets nestle in silos up to two inches deep. The jet must steer through even the narrowest passages cautiously, in case a rocket takes off right under it.

j. Sector Five requires the most precise maneuvers of all. Horizontal passages, just wide enough to accommodate the jet, connect large caverns in which the player must fly all the way from top to bottom or back with very little horizontal room. To make matters worse, both the passages and the caverns can have rows of fuel tanks along the floor.

If the jet tries to pass through these areas without shooting the fuel tanks in its path, it will crash.

k. At last, the base. The jet must make its way through a maze just as treacherous as the last, except this time with more than just survival as its goal. At the bottom of every canyon over which the jet flies lies the base, a large octagon with flashing lights. The base must be destroyed by bomb or laser; until a base is destroyed, the jet flies over canyon after canyon, using up fuel. When the player does manage to destroy the base, the jet starts over in Sector One.

The difficulty in destroying the base lies in the fact that the jet appears to be flying too high to reach it by laser, and the canyons are too narrow for the use of bombs. Many players do not realize, however, that the jet is dispensable once the base is destroyed. In other words, once the jet has come close enough to the base to demolish it with a bomb or laser, it can crash against a wall and still be reusable in the next round.

l. With the beginning of each round, another little flag appears at bottom right. Every round is the same as the first in every detail, with identical terrain and target deployment, except that up until the fourth flag, the fuel is consumed somewhat faster each round.

STRATEGIES

a. Always watch what passes below you as you fly, especially in Sectors One through Four.

b. Ignore the 10 points added to your score every second: you want to finish each round quickly, because running out of fuel is bad news.

Try also to hit as many fuel tanks as you can, even in preference to mystery bases. One hundred and fifty points plus fuel is more desirable than an average mystery score of 200 points.

c. When your fuel gets low, the rule is to ignore everything but speed, survival, and getting more fuel.

d. In Sector One, fly close to the ground. Your object should be scoring points rather than precise maneuvering, so keep in mind just a few simple rules:

1. Fly slowly only when you must to destroy a rich cluster of targets.

2. Release a couple of bombs just as you top each mountain, then descend quickly into the valley.

3. Once there, shoot any threatening rockets by slowing down for a second and using your laser. Descend to the lowest plateau at the earliest opportunity, shooting lasers constantly to clear your path of targets.

4. Rise with the terrain, using your laser against targets in the foothills, and go all the way up only when the next mountain forces you to.

5. After the last mountain, be prepared for the UFOs.

e. Through Sector Two, simply fly relatively low at medium speed, pressing LASER and BOMB constantly. The laser shots will take care of almost all the UFOs in your way. If one or two survive until you reach them, shift to full speed until you pass them, dodging vertically if necessary.

Try to time the release of your bombs so that they hit fuel tanks, compensating for your middling speed.

f. Don't try to stay alive among the fireballs. Staying below them makes sense for two reasons—you keep your jet, and you even have a chance to pick up some points from the sparse targets below.

As for making it from valley to valley, just go where the fireballs aren't. Fly quickly through each valley, then stop just before you leave shelter. Wait there until a fireball passes just over you; then chances are that you will have a second in which to duck swiftly over and into the next valley. You will find there is definitely a rhythm to it.

g. If you fly through the city too fast, you might not be able to react in time to a juicy cluster of targets or to a rocket rising in your path. Fly at medium speed, lasering and bombing for all you are worth, especially at rockets in front of you and fuel tanks beneath you.

When you fly over silos too deep for your bombs to penetrate, accelerate for a moment in case the rockets suddenly take off toward your underside.

Treat a low roof just as you would a Sector One valley: descend and laser the row of targets into oblivion. Be careful, though, when reascending; the rises here are much more abrupt than in Sector One.

h. Without excellent vertical control, you will never make it through Sector Five. Blasting away the fuel tanks blocking your path is vital but requires much less of your concentration than does piloting the jet through such a tortuous maze.

As soon as you emerge from a passageway, stop. Then move up or down, whichever you need, as far as you can until the screen catches up with you and pushes you forward. Keep the joystick to the left; while the screen propels you, you should have time to find just the right height for entering the next passage.

Once you are in the next passage, speed up right away, giving yourself a head start for the next cavern; you will have to stop once again when you enter it. The cycle requires concentration even once you know the rhythm.

Sometimes, you will enter a cavern at top left and need to leave it through a passage at bottom right, but fuel tanks will block the mouth of the passage, cluttering even the cavern floor. If you are worried about crashing into these tanks from above before you have a chance to laser them, just drop a couple of bombs at the right moment in your descent. The tanks will stand in your way no longer.

i. Once you know its secrets, the base may actually be slightly easier than Sector Five. To destroy the enemy octagon, all you have to do is gun your engine before you enter its canyon, then pull sharply down and back, and nose up to it. If you are on its level, fire your laser; if just above, drop a bomb. You will destroy the base.

You will also crash your own ship, but no matter: you will start the next round with a free replacement. Most players are afraid of crashing, so they fly too high for their bombs to have any hope of reaching the base. Eventually, they crash or run out of fuel.

j. By now, you have probably realized the one step essential to mastering SCRAMBLE: memorization. Since the pattern repeats itself every round, being prepared for upcoming opportunities and dangers is what the game is all about.

15. SPACE FURY

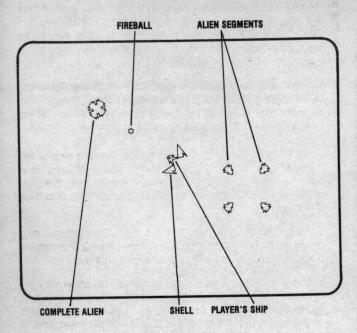

FIREBALL · ALIEN SEGMENTS

COMPLETE ALIEN · SHELL · PLAYER'S SHIP

CONTROLS

a. Left and right ROTATE buttons

b. THRUST button

c. FIRE button

SCORING

a. Alien segment before rendezvous: 10, 20, 30, or 40 points

b. Complete alien: 20, 40, 80, or 150 points

c. Fireball: 30, 60, 100, or 200 points

d. Incomplete alien: 40, 80, 150, or 300 points

e. Bonus for each docking

f. Extra ship at 10,000 points

DANGERS

a. Collision with any complete alien, alien segment after rendezvous, or fireball destroys the player's ship.

OBSERVATIONS

a. The first four rounds of SPACE FURY each feature a different type of alien enemy; from the fifth round on, the four varieties of alien mingle. The four different values listed for each item in Scoring are for the four alien species and their fireballs.

b. Docking comes at the end of each round. The player's ship appears at center and must fly into one of three fitted shells, each with a different firing capability and color:

1. The shell at left is dark blue and fires two shots straight ahead. Whenever the player presses FIRE, therefore, a line of three bullets emerges from the front of the ship. The player can have any number of bullets on the screen at a time.

2. The shell at top is green and fires one bullet to each side.

3. The shell at right is light blue and fires two bullets straight behind.

c. The operator chooses a time limit for docking, from 3 to 11 seconds; however, if the player knows which shell he wants, rotating and thrusting should take one second at most.

Successful docking brings the player two benefits:

1. His bonus from the previous round. The bonus always starts at 5,000 points and decreases by 100 per second until all aliens on the screen have bitten the dust. After 50 seconds, when it reaches 0, the round ends even if the player has not yet exterminated all the aliens.

2. A new shell for the next round. When the player uses one shell to complete a round within 50 seconds, it vanishes forever. At the end of two successful rounds, for instance, the player has only two shells to pick from during docking.

When he does not finish a round within 50 seconds, he begins the next round with the same shell.

d. When the player's ship is destroyed in the middle of a round, he must start the round over with the same shell. The bonus returns to 5,000.

e. The aliens are sparse at the beginning of each round but become increasingly numerous. Once reinforcements start pouring in, it becomes more and more difficult to finish the round in time.

f. Aliens first appear in quarters. The quarters materialize on the screen and immediately head toward one another, all four meeting simultaneously at right angles. Rounds always start with at least eight quarters meeting in two places.

When a quarter passes through the player's ship on its way to a rendezvous, neither is affected. As soon as the rendezvous is made, the ship and the alien both explode on impact.

g. If all four quarters make it to the rendezvous, the complete alien begins moving slowly in a random direction. Like the player's ship, aliens can always travel behind the screen.

Complete aliens have the ability to generate fireballs, which they launch straight at the player's ship. The fireballs, red six-pointed stars, tumble in straight lines and can harm the player only if they hit the ship itself (not the shell, which they pass through).

h. When the player manages to shoot one, two, or three quarters before the rendezvous, the surviving portion of the alien is still dangerous. It cannot launch fireballs, but it does begin a lethal tumble toward the player's ship. Unlike the fireballs, the incomplete aliens turn to track the player's ship as it moves until they are destroyed.

i. Reinforcements appear almost immediately from the fourth round on, so it is just about impossible to score any bonus. From then on, the 5,000 points serve only as a timer; each round lasts 50 seconds. The player's shell in the fourth round will be his shell from then on.

STRATEGIES

a. Shoot aliens and segments as quickly as you can. Not only will you receive a larger bonus for finishing faster, but you will score many points per second during the round.

b. The reason for ending the first and second rounds quickly is simple: there is no way you can score 100 points per second, and you are losing that many.

   By the third round, you might be able to get 100 per second, but you want to finish in time so that you can dock for the third and last time.

   From the fourth round on, you have no choice but to take 50 seconds. Shooting quickly becomes less a matter of score than of survival.

c. I find the shell on the right the most powerful because it concentrates all fire in one direction. Next in potential is the one on the left, which fires two bullets in one direction. Least useful is the green shell, since it makes you aim in three directions at once.

   Because the rounds increase in difficulty, use the green shell first, and save the dark blue for last. You will need it, so you must finish the third round in time.

d. When alien quarters materialize, try to shoot at least one from each set of four: shooting a segment and an incomplete alien is worth more than twice what you get from shooting a complete alien; an incomplete alien is a larger and less dangerous attacker than a fireball.

e. If a complete alien does form, shoot it before it can generate any fireballs. Once it launches one, you must thrust out of the fireball's path. Try shooting it, but don't stand still once it gets close.

From the third round on, thrust becomes increasingly important to survival, but use it sparingly; you aim better when you
are in control. Anyone with ASTEROIDS experience should
have little trouble maneuvering in SPACE FURY.

f. When incomplete aliens threaten you, they are large
enough for you to shoot without bothering to aim precisely,
especially once they are close. Your main concerns should
always be the prevention and extermination of complete
aliens.

16. SPACE ODYSSEY

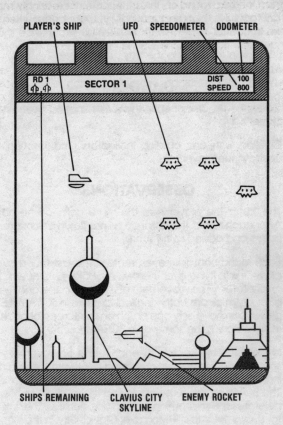

PLAYER'S SHIP UFO SPEEDOMETER ODOMETER

RD 1

SECTOR 1

DIST 100
SPEED 800

SHIPS REMAINING CLAVIUS CITY SKYLINE ENEMY ROCKET

CONTROLS

a. Four-directional joystick

b. BOMB button

c. LASER button

SCORING

a. There are many different enemy vessels in SPACE ODYSSEY;

91

most of their values consist of a base score, usually O, plus 100 points in the first round, 200 in the second, and so on. Exceptions are noted in the observations.

b. Bonus ship for beating the day's high score

DANGERS

a. Collision with any enemy ship or its missiles destroys the player's ship.

b. Collision with any building in Sectors One through Four destroys the player's ship.

OBSERVATIONS

a. The faster the player flies, the more distance he covers. After each round, the distance he has flown is converted to points and added to his score.

b. Each round contains seven sectors. The first four show the player's ship flying over the skyline of Clavius City, which he must protect. The movement of the landscape and the use of the joystick are both identical to those in SCRAMBLE. The player can have only one bomb on the screen at once, but its trajectory is the same as in SCRAMBLE.

In the last three sectors of each round, however, the perspective changes to an overhead view, with the ship moving and firing vertically on the screen instead of horizontally. The BOMB button is useless. Pulling the joystick up now accelerates the ship; pulling it down decelerates. The fifth sector shows the ship still flying over Clavius City; in the sixth and seventh, the ship is in outer space.

c. If the player's ship is destroyed, its replacement must start the sector over.

d. In Sector One, the player must fly through a fleet of UFOs that neither shoot nor maneuver. The only threat, a slight one, is the series of rockets weaving among the buildings during the first three sectors. They sometimes turn at a right angle directly towards the player's ship.

Throughout the first four sectors, larger ships cruise below the skyline. They pose no threat at all, but bombing them can be rewarding, since they have random base scores from O up.

e. Sector Two features enemies that rise in front of the player's ship and try to ram it. They fly beneath the skyline from right to left, then rise to top right. The higher the player flies, the later they reach his level, the further they are horizontally when they do, and the more time he has to react.

f. Mothership Galactica appears in Sector Three; she is long but not very wide. She fires once in a while from two gunports at her tip; meanwhile, she releases a constant stream of small modules from her stern. They spread up and down across the screen like a wake behind her.

All the player has to do is fly past the Galactica, but she does have a base score of 200 points. To destroy her, he must score eight hits, either laser or bombs or both.

g. The long, thin enemy ships in Sector Four are aligned vertically but fly and fire straight from right to left, occasionally shooting simultaneously from both ends. When one is shot in the midsection, the only vulnerable part, the midsection disappears, but the rest of the ship remains.

The player can score 100 points in the first round, 200 in the second, and so on, by flying through the gap he has created in one of these vessels, but he must look out for missiles from the next ones. If he crashes into either of the end segments of a dead ship, moreover, he is done for.

One or two of the enemies fly along the top of the screen with just their midsections and lower end segments showing. The midsections are too near the top for the player's laser to hit them.

h. In Sector Five, enemy rockets fly down the screen without firing, although their number makes them hard to avoid. The overhead view of Clavius City has several black spaces, but there is nothing wrong with flying over them.

i. Up to six enemies can be on the screen at once during Sector Six. They always stay at the top of the screen, weaving back and forth and aiming their shots at the player's ship. He must fly a certain distance to survive the sector.

Black holes appear randomly throughout the sector. If the player gets too close to one, he temporarily loses all steering ability; although he can still fire, he is a sitting duck.

j. In Sector Seven, he must make it through a shower of indestructible meteors. They are difficult to dodge, but there is always a relatively clear passageway on the left.

k. The rewards increase in each round, and the player has a higher and higher maximum speed; unfortunately, his minimum speed increases too, and all his enemies accelerate accordingly. Everything gets harder.

STRATEGIES

a. Fly fast whenever you can; in addition to scoring distance points, you can avoid slow-flying enemies.

b. Fly slowly through Sector One, moving up and down to eliminate as many UFOs as possible. The points they give you will compensate for the distance points you lose.

Look out for tall buildings and rockets from below; bomb mystery ships when you can.

c. Fly high and slowly during Sector Two, shooting constantly; the one or two ships that escape your fire will be easy to dodge by an accelerated swerve.

d. Watch out for the Galactica's fire while you fire your laser at it; if you get in enough shots before you reach it, the bombs you drop on it should finish it off. Look out for the wake of modules behind; shooting as you bomb will score points and ensure your safety.

Since the Galactica appears at your height, descend to the middle of the screen and start firing as soon as you finish Sector Two.

e. Move up and down again during Sector Four, shooting almost all the midsections and flying through as many gaps as possible.

f. You will need speed and concentration to pass through more than a few without crashing, but constant firing will knock out incoming ships without your having to aim. Avoid the bottom halves at the top of the screen.

After Sector Four, you have about a second to adopt a vertical frame of reference. Do so.

g. Ignore Clavius City in Sector Five. There is no reason not to fly fast, but fire all the time. For more points, shift back and forth quickly to eliminate all rockets in an area about four inches across.

h. Fly fast through the next sector as well; otherwise, you'll be in it longer. Since the enemy craft aim at you, you must constantly move from side to side.

Black holes are death, so fly up the center. When one appears in front of you, it is easier to avoid than it would be if you were on the side.

i. Find the meteor-free corridor on the left and stay there as long as you can; outside it, you need very quick reflexes. In later rounds, you must gear yourself for higher speeds all around.

17. STAR CASTLE

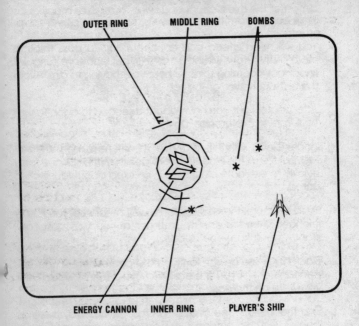

OUTER RING   MIDDLE RING   BOMBS

ENERGY CANNON   INNER RING   PLAYER'S SHIP

CONTROLS

a. Left and right ROTATE buttons

b. THRUST button

c. FIRE button

SCORING

a. Outer ring: 10 points per side destroyed

b. Middle ring: 20 points per side destroyed

c. Inner ring: 30 points per side destroyed

d. Bonus plus extra ship for each cannon destroyed

DANGERS

a. Small bombs from the castle walls destroy the player's ship on impact.

b. Center cannon shoots lethal fireballs.

OBSERVATIONS

a. The player's ship can shoot in bursts of three and travel behind the screen. Whenever it strikes the outer boundaries of the castle, whether or not there are any walls there, it automatically rebounds in the opposite direction.

b. The three "energy rings" of the castle are actually dodecagons. The twelve sides of each ring must be hit twice to be destroyed; after the first time, they glow to show they have been hit.

   Two of the rings turn quickly in different directions, and the third turns slowly. Whenever the outer ring is completely destroyed, the middle and inner ones enlarge and move out, and a new one forms around the cannon. Since the player's main goal is to destroy the cannon, he must shoot selectively.

c. The central cannon's barrel always follows the player's ship around the screen, slowly at first. Whenever gaps in all three rings pass before the barrel at once, it takes advantage of the opportunity by releasing a fireball. Because the barrel usually points to the player's ship, the ship is often in the path of the fireball.

   When the cannon is hit, the player receives a bonus ship and credit for all the ring segments remaining in the castle.

d. Like the fireball, the bombs cannot pass behind the screen, as the player's ship and its missiles can.

   There are never more than three bombs on the screen at once. They pass from the inner ring to the middle to the outer and then into space, where they track the player's ship. The ship can destroy them with missiles, but they bring no points.

e. As time passes, whether cannons are destroyed or not, everything speeds up. The bombs become faster than the spaceship, the rings revolve more quickly, and the cannon no longer merely turns to face the ship when the player emerges from behind the screen; it blinks into position.

STRATEGIES

a. Get used to using the edges of the screen. It will come in handy once you start using the patterns set forth below, and it's always a good habit in ASTEROIDS-type games.

b. After a certain point in the game, you must learn never to stay in one place for more than a second.

c. It's a shame that the game speeds up with time instead of with each cannon destroyed; otherwise, you could play indefinitely simply by destroying the first castle's outer ring over and over. As it is, though, you must take as little time as possible to destroy each castle, ensuring a steady supply of bonus ships.

d. Except for shifting the slow ring to the middle later in the game (see Strategy i), try not to let a castle grow new rings. It wastes time.

e. Similarly, shoot an approaching bomb only if it is alone and you do not want to move. Otherwise, you are wasting your time, gaining no points, and taking the risk of missing.

f. When you have only the inner ring between you and the cannon and you are close enough, a triple burst will destroy it before it has a chance to retaliate.

g. When the game begins to speed up, try this simple pattern: go to the center of the left or right edge and face the edge of the screen. Your shots will cross behind and hit the other side of the castle.

At soon as the bombs get too close for comfort, simply thrust about an inch forward and you will be on the other side of the screen, still firing at the castle. As the bombs cross the screen towards you, turn around and repeat the procedure.

h. Once the game is at maximum speed, you will need a more sophisticated technique. Here it is:

Spend all your time in two opposite corners. You should dart back and forth behind the screen, developing a turn-thrust--shoot rhythm and synchronizing it with the outer ring so that you are always shooting at the same spot. Once you perfect this method, the cannon and bombs will never be fast enough to do more than almost destroy you.

i. For best effect, the corner pattern should be followed with the slow ring in the middle. You can shift it to this position by quickly destroying the outer wall twice before beginning your attack in earnest.

6
MAZE GAMES

18. ARMOR ATTACK

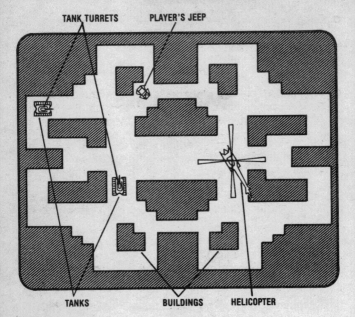

TANK TURRETS   PLAYER'S JEEP

TANKS   BUILDINGS   HELICOPTER

CONTROLS

a. Left and right ROTATE buttons

b. FORWARD button

c. FIRE button

SCORING

a. Tank body: 20 points

b. Tank turret: 30 points plus bonus

c. Helicopter: 50 points plus advance turret bonus by 10

d. When turret bonus reaches 50, player receives an extra jeep, and bonus is reset

DANGERS

a. Being shot by any tank or helicopter destroys the jeep.

b. Colliding with any tank destroys the jeep.

OBSERVATIONS

a. The buildings are superimposed on the screen, so the tanks and helicopters act as though they were not there at all. The player, however, can always use them for shelter.

b. Tanks move to reach the jeep, but the buildings often hinder them. Their turrets move independently, turning to aim and fire at the jeep.

c. The jeep's first hit on a tank immobilizes it but has no effect on the turret, which still turns and fires until it is immobilized in turn.

Once a tank is entirely destroyed, the jeep still must not touch it. The tanks appear several at a time, so that there are always a few wrecks for the jeep to bypass by the time the wave ends.

d. Helicopters, on the other hand, appear one at a time at regular intervals but from randomly chosen sides of the screen. A helicopter shoots quickly straight ahead, homing in on the jeep immediately; it is not hindered by the buildings, although the player can use them as shelter against its bullets.

To destroy a helicopter, the player must shoot it as he would a tank (three dimensions yield here to two). When hit the helicopter explodes brightly, but neither tank nor jeep in its vicinity is injured; a tank explosion is also harmless.

e. Because the player keeps receiving bonus jeeps by shooting helicopters, the game would go on forever if the play did not become more difficult—and it does, with the tanks becoming smarter, faster, and more numerous.

STRATEGIES

a. The buildings are your allies. Use them well.

b. Wait behind corners for tanks that are tracking you, then blast them twice and retreat in case the turrets are still functional.

c. Watch the turret of each tank on the screen to predict where it will shoot next. If you move fast enough, you can sneak up on them from behind in the early rounds.

d. Other strategies are common to several maze games:

    1. Lure one tank between you and another. The one in the middle will be destroyed by its comrade's shells, especially since the first will immobilize it. You get the points.

    2. Guerrilla tactics are best whenever you are outnumbered. Never venture out in the open, stay away from groups, and pick your enemies off one at a time, taking your time about it.

e. Dealing with helicopters is simple enough once you have the knack. As soon as one appears, just put a building between it and you. Aim at the helicopter; when it is almost right over you, fire. Score 50 points and add 10 to the turret bonus.

    If you try to shoot it out in the open, you may win, but chances are that you won't, since you lack the cover of a building.

f. Steer clear of tanks even when you have destroyed them.

19. BERZERK

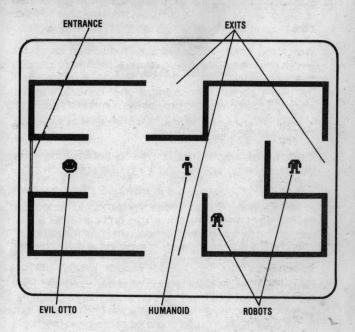

ENTRANCE   EXITS

EVIL OTTO   HUMANOID   ROBOTS

CONTROLS

a. Eight-directional joystick

b. FIRE button

SCORING

a. Robot: 50 points

b. Bonus for shooting all robots in a maze: 10 points per robot

c. Extra humanoid at 5,000 points

DANGERS

a. All walls are death to touch.

b. Robots shoot bullets; if the humanoid is hit, he dies.

c. If the humanoid collides with a robot or Evil Otto, he dies.

OBSERVATIONS

a. The game consists of one maze after another, each of which can be completed only by the humanoid's death or escape. Sixty-four thousand different mazes are possible, so chances of repetition are low.

b. The humanoid's motion and aim are controlled by the same joystick, so he cannot run and fire in different directions simultaneously.

c. At the beginning of each maze, the humanoid appears at the middle of one of the four edges and can escape only through the middle of another side. In the next maze, he appears on the side opposite his last exit. In the meantime, he can fire about two bullets per second.

d. From 4 to 12 robots appear soon after the humanoid. They are his enemies. Like him, they can shoot in eight directions. They shoot whenever he is in their sights and move so that he will be. If the humanoid and a robot are separated by a wall segment, for example, and the humanoid walks to one end of the segment and past it, the robot will follow him step by step, shooting at him all the while.

e. The robots are not too smart. They are often destroyed not by the humanoid's bullets but by walking into walls, walking into one another, shooting one another, or being zapped by Evil Otto. No matter how they die, the player gets the credit.

f. Evil Otto is a smiling ball that bounces out from wherever the humanoid began that maze. He appears after about ten seconds and immediately pursues the humanoid, bouncing along horizontally or vertically toward his prey. The bounces are about two inches high, slow while robots remain on the screen and faster once the robots all die. If the humanoid moves, Otto shifts course accordingly.

g. Diagonal bullets are the hardest to dodge.

h. When a robot dies, it disappears by explosion. If the humanoid shoots a robot pointblank and then walks into the explosion, he dies as well.

i. When the robots appear, the player has one second or less before they start shooting at him.

j. Occcasionally, a player must dodge a bullet at the beginning of the maze and accidentally backs into the side from which he emerged, now a deadly wall. Blind reflex does not always produce the best results.

k. There·are two models of BERZERK out, each with a different way of getting harder. The old model has:

   1. Yellow robots without bullets

   2. Red robots shooting one at a time

   3. White robots shooting two at a time

After 5,000 points, Otto travels twice as fast. In the new model there are:

   1. Yellow robots without bullets

   2. Red robots shooting one at a time

   3. White robots shooting two at a time

   4. Purple robots shooting three at a time

   5. Yellow robots shooting four at a time

   6. Purple robots shooting five at a time

   7. White robots shooting one superfast bullet at a time.

and so on up to five superfast bullets at a time, but Otto always moves slowly.

STRATEGIES

a. When you complete one maze, start getting ready for the next.

b. Learn to use the controls; if your hands do not react instantly to your thoughts, you will have trouble staying alive.

c. Because of the time pressure and for purposes of self-defense, shoot whenever you have a target.

d. Once you realize how the robots move and shoot, it should not be difficult to deal with them singly. Try to stay clear of gangs, though, since you can't cover yourself in more than one direction at a time. If you do end up surrounded—at the beginning of a maze, for instance—shoot your way out and run. The farther you are from your enemies, the more time you have to dodge their shots.

If you want to demolish a large group of robots in a short time, either shoot at them from far away or put a wall between yourself and them. As you pass the end of the wall, they will follow you from cover. Pick them off one by one as they emerge, being sure to dodge any shots they have a chance to fire.

e. Keep in mind that you need not kill all the robots with your own bullets. Here are a few ways to have them meet other deaths:

1. If you are between two distant robots and both shoot at you, step out of the way for a moment while the bullets go by. Since the robots will follow you, you must then step back into the line of fire. They will do the same and be destroyed without your firing a shot.

2. If you are near a lone robot, you can influence him by your movements to walk into a wall. It doesn't take long.

3. If two robots are near each other on the other side of a wall from you, move back and forth rapidly, trying to draw each in the direction of the other. They will probably collide and both be destroyed.

4. If you are running out of time and must choose between shooting robots in one corner of the maze and shooting robots in the center, go to the corner. Then, when Otto appears, your presence will draw him across the center, so the survivors will die before you escape.

If the only robots left are not in the center but out of your range when Otto appears, do what you can to make him zap them. It can be done if you pick the right place to wait.

f. Otto is the timer, making a leisurely pace unwise. If you use him as outlined above, wait just inside the maze and exit as soon as there is nothing more to be gained. At his fastest, he can easily outrun you.

g. When you have a choice of robots to shoot, start with diagonal shots. You will, thus, avoid being the target of diagonal fire, the most dangerous of all.

If a robot does manage to get the drop on you and shoot diagonally, the best dodge is another diagonal move, but perpendicular to the course of the bullet. A vertical or horizontal evasion would require you to travel a longer distance before you were safe.

h. Do not assume that you can walk through a robot with impunity if you have just shot it. The explosion could kill you.

i. At the beginning of each maze, especially later in the game, know where you will appear and be prepared for shots from any distance and direction. Good players lose more humanoids at the beginning than at any other point in the maze.

j. Start shooting right away; if you must dodge, resist the natural tendency to retreat into the wall you just emerged from.

k. Recognize any change in the color of your enemies; before they shoot a single bullet, you will know that their firepower has increased.

20. PAC-MAN

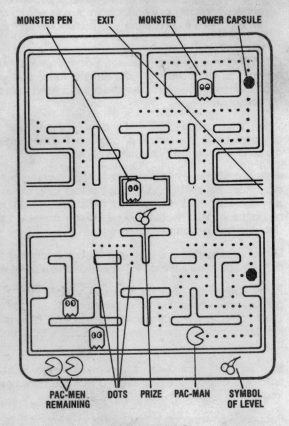

MONSTER PEN   EXIT   MONSTER   POWER CAPSULE

PAC-MEN REMAINING   DOTS   PRIZE   PAC-MAN   SYMBOL OF LEVEL

CONTROLS

a. Four-directional joystick

SCORING

a. Dot: 10 points

b. Power capsule: 50 points

c. Blue monster: 200, 400, 800, or 1,600 points

d. Prizes

      Screen 1: 100 points

      Screen 2: 300 points

      Screen 3: 500 points

      Screen 4: 700 points

      Screen 5: 1,000 points

      Screen 6: 2,000 points

e. Bonus Pac-Man at 10,000 points

DANGERS

a. If the Pac-Man collides with any of the four monsters when they are their regular colors, he is a goner.

OBSERVATIONS

a. Each screen ends as soon as the Pac-Man has devoured all 240 dots and the four power capsules. He travels more slowly when he is eating dots than when he is not.

b. Four monsters, Inky, Blinky, Pinky, and Clyde, emerge from their pen at center to pursue the Pac-Man. Their eyes roll to face whichever directions they are traveling in.

The monsters travel at first in predetermined patterns that may vary only slightly from screen to screen. As soon as any one "sees" the Pac-Man–that is, as soon as one is moving toward him in the same corridor, so its eyes are toward him– it begins to chase him.

Chasing basically entails this: at each intersection, the monster asks the computer, "What is the best route to reach him now?" The program then sends it in that direction. The red monster is slightly faster than its comrades.

It is very difficult to lay down concrete rules for PAC-MAN. Exceptions do continually occur, and the player must be ready for them. Sometimes, for instance, reversing over and over confuses the monsters and makes them lose the trail. There are also different versions of the game out (see Observation h).

c. The maze always has a few safe spots: the two exits and the area just above the monsters' pen. In the early screens, pursuers slow down when going through the exits and lose some of their tracking ability above the monsters' pen.

d. When the Pac-Man eats a power capsule, the monsters suddenly turn blue and start to flee instead of pursue, for he is now more powerful than they.

The first one he catches after each power capsule gives him 200 points; the second, 400; the third, 800; and the fourth, 1,600. When he catches one, its eyes make a disembodied beeline back to the pen, where they receive new bodies and quickly reemerge.

After a short time, the remaining blue monsters flash four times, returning to their normal colors and capabilities after the fourth flash.

e. Monsters cannot harm the Pac-Man until they are all the way out of their pen, which he can never enter.

f. At the beginning of each screen, one more symbol appears under the maze to the right. This symbol becomes the prize, appearing below the monsters' pen twice, staying for a while for the Pac-Man to clear it, and then disappearing each time if he does not.

g. The prize in the first screen is always cherries; in the second, a strawberry; and in the third, a peach. Next come more fruits, chosen randomly; then, assorted bells, medals, and keys; then a series of gold and silver bars.

There exist several different skill levels, determined by the monsters' speed and sophistication; what many players do not realize is that the skill level for each screen is signaled by the prize. Mazes with apples for prizes, for example, always present the same level of challenge.

For each skill level, the player needs a different strategic pattern. The monsters become much smarter and faster and are affected less and less by the power capsules. In mazes with silver bars, they move half again as fast as the Pac-Man and do not even flash, let alone turn blue, when he eats a power capsule. The instant one sees him, moreover, they **all** start tracking him, working as a team to cut him off.

h. Once the player learns the games's patterns, he can make one quarter last a long time. I have heard of scores as high as 1,300,000. Arcade owners are not very happy about this development, so there has been a rash of fiendish new programs designed to shorten playing time. These additions can speed up the action, change the monsters' routine movements to make the old patterns obsolete, or even make the monsters move randomly.

STRATEGIES

a. Keep out of the monsters' sight for as long as possible while you clear dots; you can travel more quickly when most of the dots are gone. So that you won't have to waste time retracing your steps, try to eat all the dots in each corridor you enter.

Once one or more monsters are on your trail, don't make U-turns, since they will take shortcuts after you. You can usually shake them by going through a side exit, losing them in the safe spot above their pen, or making a few fake reverses. Once three or more are after you, head for a power capsule.

b. Save the power capsules for last, when you can concentrate on catching the monsters. Wait until at least three are nearby before you eat a capsule, since they will try to disperse when you do.

When only one power capsule and a few dots on either side of it remain, do not eat them all at once. If you do, the screen will end before you can catch any blue monsters.

c. If you are trapped between two monsters, you have no hope unless one is looking the other way, in which case you should follow it to safety.

d. If you can, watch the eyes of every monster in the maze so that you can keep track of their movements and avoid them.

e. Try to collect the prize both times in every screen. The more valuable they become, the less sense it makes to travel through the maze fruitlessly.

f. Without learning some patterns, you will need a great deal of skill to get far at all. The best way to learn is to watch good players; developing your own patterns is fine, too, but usually an unnecessary investment.

You will need different patterns for each skill level, usually variations on the original one. In later screens, your patterns will have to include more evasive action and shorter forays for blue monsters.

The only problem with patterns is that, after you go to the trouble of learning them, the machine you have been playing may be given a new program. If your patterns become obsolete, you must either find another machine with the original program or devise new patterns, if possible, for the machine you have been playing.

21. RALLY-X

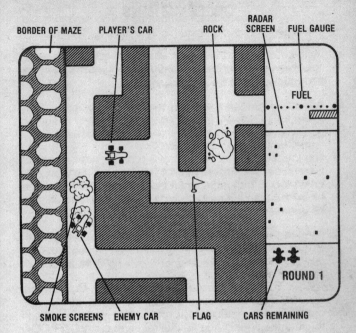

BORDER OF MAZE   PLAYER'S CAR   ROCK   RADAR SCREEN   FUEL GAUGE

FUEL

ROUND 1

SMOKE SCREENS   ENEMY CAR   FLAG   CARS REMAINING

CONTROLS

a. Four-directional joystick

b. SMOKE SCREEN button

SCORING

a. Flag: 100-2,000 points

b. Bonus at end of each round for fuel remaining

DANGERS

a. Collision with any crash car or rock destroys the player's car.

b. If the player loses all his cars or runs out of fuel, the game ends.

OBSERVATIONS

a. The player is in a large maze, only a small portion of which shows on the screen at any moment.

b. The first maze is the same in every game except for its flags; the later mazes differ slightly each time.

c. Rocks are placed here and there in every maze. They destroy the player's car on impact but merely block the movements of the crash cars.

d. The radar screen to the right of the big picture represents the entire maze, except that it shows none of the walls, only colored dots that represent flags and cars (not rocks). The player can use the radar to know where he is in relation to his enemies and his objectives.

e. Each maze contains 10 flags, all of which must be cleared to complete the maze. The flag with the "S" next to it is the special one, although the radar shows no difference.

The first flag in each maze gives the player 100 points; the second, 200; and so on, except that every one counts double from the special flag on. If the player is lucky enough to clear the special flag first, he receives a total of 11,000 points; if he clears it last, he gets only 6,500.

f. The crash cars track the player relentlessly, except when he leaves a smoke screen behind him. They then lose his trail temporarily. The only drawback is that smoke screens consume fuel.

g. The player begins each round with a new fuel supply. The rounds get harder by featuring more or faster cars. For instance, in the first four rounds:

1. Three slow cars

2. Three fast cars

3. Eight slow cars

4. Eight fast cars

It becomes very hard to clear all ten flags before crashing or running out of fuel.

STRATEGIES

a. As soon as you clear one flag, go on to the next. Even if you're not worried about using up your fuel, think of the bonus at the end of the round.

b. Learn the first maze well. In the upper right, for instance, it might benefit you to know of a loop to stay out of when two or more cars are pursuing you, lest they cooperate to trap you.

c. If you see two flags on the big screen and one of them is the special, clear it first.

d. Use the radar to plot your route, although you must always keep an eye on the big screen for rocks, turns, and flags.

e. Learn that the crash cars track you by where you are, not by where you are going. Evading them is usually pretty easy, so use smoke screens only in emergencies.

f. If you are familiar with how the game gets harder, you'll be much better prepared for the new and fast crash cars.

22. TARG

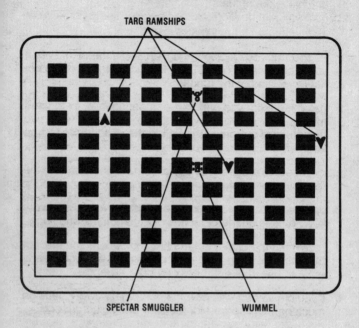

TARG RAMSHIPS

SPECTAR SMUGGLER   WUMMEL

CONTROLS

a. Four-directional joystick

b. FIRE button

SCORING

a. Ramship: 10+ points

b. Smuggler: 100-900 points

c. Bonus at end of each screen

d. Extended play for beating day's high score

DANGERS

a. Collision with any ramship or smuggler destroys the Wummel.

OBSERVATIONS

a. The screen is a grid of corridors through which the player's Wummel and its enemies, the Spectar smugglers and the Targ ramships, move.

b. The Wummel turns quickly to the right or left but must decelerate before reversing. It can have one shot on the screen at a time, shooting in the same direction it is moving.

c. Ten Targ ramships appear at the beginning of each round. They all want to ram the Wummel, which tries to shoot them. Unfortunately, they are reluctant to be in front of him in any corridor, turning away as soon as they can. They do like chasing him, though.

d. As time passes within a round, the ramships become faster.

e. One Spectar smuggler at a time, having a random value, also pursues the Wummel. When one smuggler is destroyed, one of the blocks of the grid becomes hollow, soon releasing the next smuggler.

f. At the end of each round, the Targ ramships' value is raised by 10 points, and the player receives a bonus of 1,000 points after the first round, 2,000 after the second, and so forth. The villains do, however, gain more speed and cunning with each round.

STRATEGIES

a. If you need to reverse quickly, turn twice. Your first turn should be into a block or the side of the maze, and your second will produce an about-face.

b. Since the ramships will never want to be in front of you for more than a moment at most, you must almost always take them by surprise.

c. It is easier to ambush one at a time than several, so use guerrilla tactics unless you are trapped.

d. When you materialize at bottom right, go two or three columns to the left and rise, shooting.

e. When an enemy is about to cross your path but you think it might ram you, slow down and get ready to shoot. Your ability to accelerate and decelerate is something the bad guys don't have.

f. When you are being pursued, turn away, turn again after one block, and immediately reverse, surprising your enemy when it reaches the second corner.

g. Whenever a smuggler is near you, find a way to shoot it. Try always to have one or two targets in mind; the sooner you finish the round, the less time your enemies will have to speed up. Be ready for tougher enemies with each succeeding round.

h. TARG is one game in which strategy must become almost reflex as the action quickens.

23. VENTURE

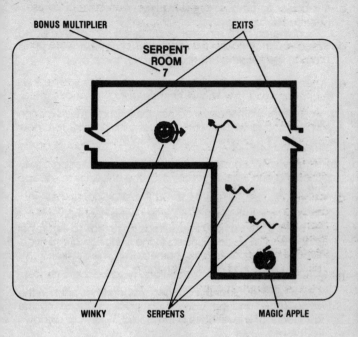

BONUS MULTIPLIER   EXITS

SERPENT
ROOM
7

WINKY   SERPENTS   MAGIC APPLE

CONTROLS

a. Eight-directional joystick

b. Fire button

SCORING

There are too many different point values in VENTURE to list individually here. In general, the scoring is as follows:

a. Hall monster: low score

b. Dungeon monster: medium score

c. Dungeon treasure: high score

d. Extra bow after clearing Level Two

DANGERS

a. Touching any hall monster or dungeon monster, or being crushed or otherwise done in, causes immediate death to Winky, the heroic archer controlled by the player.

OBSERVATIONS

a. As in several other maze games, the joystick directs motion and shooting; whenever the player shifts his bow to a new direction, he begins to move that way as well.

b. Hall monsters wander outside the dungeons, starting slowly. Shooting one will not destroy it, so the only way to escape them as they home in is to evade them.

c. To keep a treasure, Winky must leave the dungeon with it. If he is killed before he can, the treasure reverts to its original place and all dead monsters in the dungeon are revived. Except for the points Winky earned during his first time in, it is as though he had never been there.

Once he does clear the dungeon, it becomes solid on the large map, and he cannot go back in. Once all the dungeons of a level have been looted, Winky climbs down to the next level.

d. Whenever Winky is killed and reborn, he takes a new bow and tramps five steps down a staircase to the bottom of whatever level he is at, slightly left of center. If he has looted the level at all, those chambers are still solid in the overhead view. Hall monsters then begin to materialize and start tracking him within two seconds.

e. After Winky has been in one dungeon for a maximum of ten seconds, a hall monster begins to materialize just outside. Once it has grown to full size, a process of about two seconds, it makes a beeline for Winky, passing straight through whatever walls or monsters lie in its path.

If Winky leaves when he sees a hall monster outside, the monster will rarely be there when he gets out.

f. Whenever Winky leaves a dungeon and then reenters it, whatever monsters he has killed inside are alive again. If he left to flee a hall monster, furthermore, the monster will begin to rematerialize right away. The longer Winky takes going in and out, the more hall monsters will be waiting for him outside when he finally leaves.

g. Occasionally, a hall monster is waiting just outside a dungeon door, and Winky doesn't have a chance.

h. Each dungeon monster, dead or alive, is deadly to touch. Corpses disintegrate slowly, and even the last dot of color will kill Winky if he touches it.

Shooting a disintegrating corpse does not hasten its disappearance; rather, it reconstitutes the body, as though the monster has been freshly killed.

i. Dungeon monsters often seem to sense when Winky is aiming at them, and they move out of his line of fire. To shoot them, he must move, aim, and fire quickly.

It is often possible to obtain and keep a treasure just by dodging the monsters, thus saving the time it would take to kill them.

j. With the completion of each level, his total score is increased by the number of points Winky earned while there multiplied by a one-digit number displayed just under the title over the map of the level. If he gained 1,000 points in the first level, for example, they might be multiplied by 7, making his overall score 8,000.

The more time Winky takes to finish the level, the smaller the bonus multiplier becomes.

k There are too many dungeons to give a detailed description of each one, but here are previews of the first two levels, the most useful to know:

l. Level One, top left (The Wall Room): The easiest of the dungeons. Four red walls slowly move in and out; there is a diamond in the center. Winky can touch the walls and survive, as long as he doesn't let them crush him against any of the dungeon walls.

If he waits until the top or bottom wall has come as far from the center as it can, he can scoot in, grab the diamond, and leave the way he came. Shooting a hole in a wall clears a more direct path, but it earns him no points and consumes valuable time.

m. Level One, top right (The Serpent Room): The three green snakes are guarding a magic apple. They always remain horizontal and do not move very fast or dangerously, so dodging or shooting them is not difficult. If Winky enters through the door in the right-hand wall, only two snakes are wriggling between him and the apple; if he enters through the other door, he must face all three.

n. Level One, bottom left and bottom right (The Goblin Room and The Skeleton Room): The three monsters in each of these dungeons are not particularly hard to deal with, although killing them takes more time than simply escaping with the treasures. Once the player knows how they move, they should not present much of a challenge either way.

o. Level Two, top left (The Two-Headed Room): This Y-shaped dungeon seems empty as Winky enters but, as soon as he touches the treasure at the bottom, four deadly crabs appear, two blocking each exit. If Winky shoots one, its corpse might block his path to freedom when the hall monster enters.

p. Level Two, top right (The Troll Room): When Winky enters this dungeon, walls stand between him and the two angry trolls who guard their treasure. After about three seconds, though, three large gaps appear in the barrier, permitting the trolls to charge through. They are the most evasive Level Two monsters.

q. Level Two, center (The Dragon Room): The four large dragons in this room are fairly easy marks, but once they die, their corpses often block Winky's path to the treasure at the apex of the triangle and back to his one exit in its base. A hall monster is bound to enter before he can leave.

r. Level Two, bottom (The Spider Room): The three red spiders are fast and hard to hit, but they are not the dungeon's greatest threat: once Winky has managed to obtain the chamber's treasure, a dancer statuette, all three spiders, alive and dead, vanish, only to be replaced by two faster, deadlier, yellow spiders, one on each side of poor Winky.

s. The next level features such attractions as The Demon Room, The Genie Room, The Bat Room, and The Cyclops Room, each challenging in its own way. In later levels:

   1. The point values and bonuses increase.

   2. The dungeons become more difficult.

   3. The hall monsters move faster.

STRATEGIES

a. If you want to change aim without moving, learn just to tap the joystick, not to jam it.

b. When pursued by hall monsters outside the dungeons, don't waste time by shooting them. Reverse direction, switch from side to side, and do whatever else you must to escape.

c. Do your best not to shoot a monster where its corpse might block your path to or from the treasure. If you do, you have no choice but to wait until it has completely disintegrated; under no circumstances should you shoot it again.

d. Because you want to get out of each dungeon quickly, you should waste no time in picking up the treasure. It can and should be done in one fluid motion; the instant you touch the loot, you should start thinking about getting out.

e. When a hall monster appears outside a dungeon, leave. Even if it is outside the room's only exit, remember that it won't be there when you get outside—although another might.

   Once the hall monster has actually entered the dungeon, the best policy is to flee in the opposite direction. If there is no exit there or if a corpse is blocking it, it is still possible in the first three levels for a skillful Winky to escape around the hall monster. It's a risk, but do it if you have to.

f. When leaving a dungeon, look out. You don't want to run straight into a waiting hall monster. The more time you've spent in the level so far, the more you should worry.

g. The question of whether to shoot dungeon monsters when you don't absolutely have to depends on two factors: speed and accuracy. If you think you can kill several in a short time, do it. Keep in mind the bonus at the end of each level, since that determines your final score. Unless you are very fast, there is no point in risking the decrease of your score by a seventh or a sixth for a few hundred points.

h. Since you start in the same place on the level each time, it makes sense to clear the dungeons nearest you first. If you can make a circuit of the level without being killed, the strategy will save time. If you are killed and have to start over, you will have to take the same long route you avoided before.

i. In The Wall Room, don't bother shooting your way through the red walls. It's a risk that earns you no points and takes more time than simply slipping around them. Since this dungeon is the easiest, it should probably be saved for last, when you need to finish quickly.

j. In The Serpent Room, send arrows down on the two lower snakes before you enter their territory. Their length will make them easy targets from that angle.

If pressed for time, enter and exit the dungeon through the door in the right wall, avoiding a confrontation with the third snake.

k. The Goblin and Skeleton Rooms should be handled according to your inclination. You can easily evade the monsters, but the points you could gain with a few parting shots should be considered.

l. Save The Two-Headed Room for the end of Level Two, since it is a very quick job once you have the secret. When you don't have time to shoot the crabs and then to wait for them to disintegrate from your path, split-second timing alone will get you out safely. The instant you touch the treasure, jam the joystick to the upper left. Each time, you will barely make it past the crabs and out the left head of the room.

A more lucrative and time-consuming method is to stay at the bottom with your treasure and wait for the crabs to drift down from the heads into the body in search of you, as they invariably do. If you shoot well, you can kill them and still leave a clear path out. If a hall monster appears before you finish, though, say goodbye to Winky.

m. As soon as you enter The Troll Room, move about an inch to the left of the entrance, staying as low as possible; aim to the upper right. As soon as the walls vanish, one goblin will come thundering down, since he doesn't sense that you're aiming at him. Diagonal shots are your best chance against any of the monsters, but the trolls are particularly tricky.

Shoot as soon as he leaves cover, then move up and get the treasure. The remaining troll will not be hard to evade if you are fast.

Whenever you do aim vertically or horizontally, the trolls will not give you a chance to hit them, holding you in stalemate until the hall monster shows up. What you must do (if you don't want to shoot diagonally) is aim in some other direction until your target has committed himself to attack. Then quickly shift your aim and fire before he has a chance to dodge.

n. You must kill almost everything in The Dragon Room; there is no room to maneuver around the dragons while they are all alive and moving. Even if you are a skillful archer, you must take special care to shoot so that you still have a clear path to and from the treasure. If you have to wait for the dragons to disintegrate before you can reach it, you might as well forget about it.

o. The red denizens of The Spider Room will always stay near the treasure in the center; they shift around it to follow you. Shoot one for best results: it takes almost no time, and you can easily snatch the treasure from only two defenders.

The instant you do, look out for the two yellow spiders. They will close in on you rapidly, and your only chance is to duck under one and escape while you still have time. Once you reach the door, a couple of arrows shot at your pursuers won't hurt.

p. With each new level, be prepared for greater and greater challenges. Try to view each dungeon creatively to find the best strategy.

VENTURE is one game in which it is not only important but vital to watch more experienced players, observing the game's many unusual problems and the different ways of handling them. Good luck!

24. WIZARD OF WOR

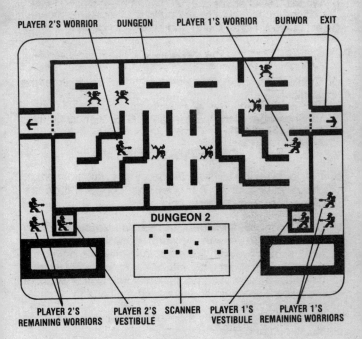

PLAYER 2'S WORRIOR   DUNGEON   PLAYER 1'S WORRIOR   BURWOR   EXIT

DUNGEON 2

PLAYER 2'S
REMAINING WORRIORS   PLAYER 2'S
VESTIBULE   SCANNER   PLAYER 1'S
VESTIBULE   PLAYER 1'S
REMAINING WORRIORS

CONTROLS

a. Four-directional joystick for each player

b. FIRE button for each player

SCORING

a. Burwor: 100 points

b. Garwor: 200 points

c. Thorwor: 500 points

d. Ally's worrior: 1,000 points

e. Worluk: 1,000 points and double score for next dungeon

129

f. Wizard: 2,500 points

g. Bonus worrior after fourth and twelfth dungeons

DANGERS

a. Collision with any worling, worluk, or wizard disintegrates the worrior.

b. Worlings shoot at the worriors, and the wizard hurls lightning bolts.

OBSERVATIONS

a. The game selects the first 7 dungeons randomly from an unchanging pool of 15. The ones from Dungeon 8 on are drawn from a much larger pool.

b. Once the money is inserted, the machine presents four play choices: one player with two worriors, one with five, two with two each, or two with five each. With only one player, the computer serves as his ally with an equal number of worriors until they all perish. A computer-controlled worrior will shoot the player's only if an enemy is on the other side.

c. Worriors buck when they shoot and can have one bullet on the screen at a time.

d. Each player's worrior enters the dungeon through a vestibule on his side of the screen. Whenever one worrior dies, the next can leave the vestibule anytime in the next ten seconds, after which he is forcibly ejected.

e. A passageway always leads from the right side of the screen to the left, sealed by a dotted line. Bullets cannot pass through this corridor, but worriors and worlings can. As soon as one does, the dotted line turns solid for about seven seconds, blocking the passageway.

f. The worlings all shoot from the second dungeon on. The blue burwors are the first to appear.

The yellow garwors and brown thorwors are more dangerous because they track the worriors and are invisible until they enter the same corridor as a worrior. The only way to keep track of them is by the scanner, which registers the movements of all the worlings in the dungeon at any time, even identifying them by colored dots. The scanner does not, however, show the walls of the dungeon.

The longer the player is in a dungeon, the faster the remaining worlings move and shoot.

g. Once all the worlings in a dungeon have died, the worluk usually appears. He flaps around trying to kill worriors or to escape through the left or right exit, whichever he can do first.

h. If the worluk is shot before it can escape, the wizard himself sometimes appears. He teleports very quickly, staying in one place only long enough to hurl a swift lightning bolt. There is no way of knowing exactly where he will appear.

i. The fourth dungeon is the Arena, so called because of the wide, clear space at center. The dungeons from the eighth on are Worlord Dungeons, with open spaces at the top. The thirteenth is called the Pit, for it has no interior walls at all. With each dungeon, the worlings are more dangerous, so the game increases in difficulty.

j. Worlings can sense where nearby worriors' guns are pointing, and they are reluctant to walk in front of one and hesitate before doing so.

Because no dungeon contains dead ends, it is usually more likely that a worling will approach a hiding worrior from behind than from ahead. Many players, however, do not realize that each dungeon has a couple of passageways that the monsters are programmed to enter from only one direction. Greg Davies of Fresno, California, supplied these diagrams:

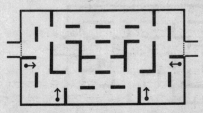

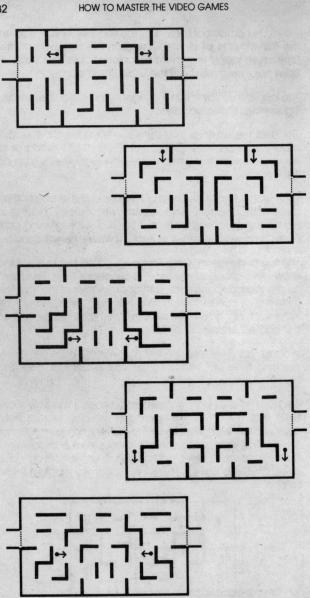

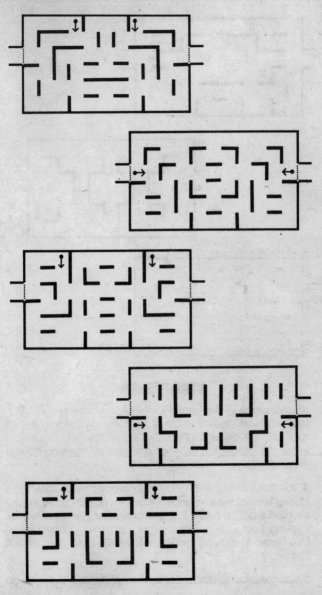

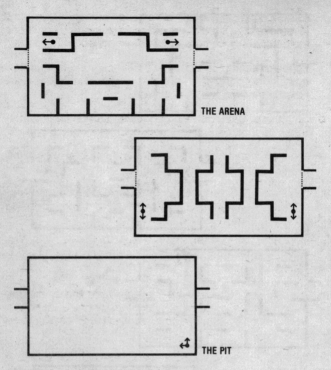

THE ARENA

THE PIT

STRATEGIES

a. Memorize all 15 dungeons that can be among the first 7,
and you won't lose a single worrior. The dungeons are not
that difficult, since many have similar layouts. Once you
know the "safe spots" in each one, you will have no trouble
dealing with your enemies.

b. If you are playing with a friend, you don't need safe spots
during the first seven dungeons, since you can position your
worriors back to back. In the Worlord Dungeons, however,
making your way to each other becomes dangerous, so
you'll have to stay on separate sides and each take on half
the worlings.

If you are playing alone, act as though the computer's worriors did not exist. They will die off soon enough. If you want to remove unwanted competition for points, you can shoot the computer's worriors for 1,000 points each.

c. In the early dungeons, to be sure that you can fire when you have to, do not shoot without a target. Later on, you will have to shoot all the time anyway.

d. Leave your vestibule as soon as the coast is clear; otherwise, you may be forced to leave when it isn't.

e. Use the left and right exits when you need an escape route or more bountiful hunting.

f. Be sure to use the scanner; know the location of every nearby worling of every color. To prevent them from speeding up too much, shoot them when you can.

g. To kill the worluk, simply wait for him by one of the exits. If he heads for the other one, walk through the first and ambush him there.

h. The only way of dealing with the wizard is to find a short corridor as soon as you kill the worluk. Stand at one end of it and fire constantly, and you might manage to hit him before he zaps you.

i. In the early dungeons, find your memorized safe spot and get there when you can, since there's no point in taking risks. For maximum points, face toward where the worlings **cannot** enter; they will soon enter where you expect, and you can quickly turn and shoot.

Later on, try to find the safe spot right away. Once there, you will have to fire constantly, because the monsters will stampede in even though you're pointing in their direction. Soon you will have to press FIRE as often as you can.

7

REFLEX GAMES

25. MONACO GP

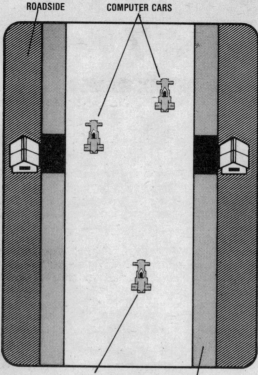

ROADSIDE COMPUTER CARS

PLAYER'S CAR BARRIER

CONTROLS

a. Steering wheel

b. Low-high gearshift

c. Gas pedal

SCORING

a. About 8 points per second in low gear with gas pedal down

b. About 25 points per second in high gear with gas pedal down

c. Extended play at 2,000 points

d. Extra cars at 4,000, 6,000, and 8,000 points

DANGERS

a. Collision with any car or wall knocks the player's car off the course.

OBSERVATIONS

a. The screen shows a road that moves from top to bottom as the player drives along it. He will crash if he hits the side of the road, but he can drive alongside it once he does. The roadside scenery does not hinder him, but he scores no points when he is not on the road.

b. Low gear keeps the car moving at a constant rate. If it starts in high gear, it begins slower than in low but then warms up and goes much faster. If the driver switches from low to high, he goes faster right away.

c. The lower the driver pushes the gas pedal, the faster he goes, according to the gear he's in.

d. If the car crashes, it spins off the road to the right and must start up again and get back on. It passes through the barrier and onto the road with no problem.

e. The car can scrape against the barrier, in which case it does not crash but slows down.

f. Puddles on the road deprive the driver of steering for a second or two.

g. Other cars appear along the course, all traveling at a speed a little lower than the player's speed in low gear. They tend to stray across the road as they drive, rebounding off the sides or changing horizontal direction at will.

h. One troublemaker is the ambulance, which first sirens and then approaches the car from behind. Regardless of gear, the car must move out of the way and let the ambulance pass.

i. Certain stretches of road are unusually difficult, such as bumpy parts; night driving, in which the driver's headlights illuminate the road for only two lengths ahead; and bottlenecks, in which the road is abruptly cut to a third or a quarter of its width. A flashing sign warns the driver of upcoming bottlenecks but, if he makes one mistake, he will either crash head-on into a wall or, if he makes it into the narrows, collide with a car ahead or behind.

j. The driver starts with 90 seconds. If he earns 2,000 points before that, he can keep driving without a timer; once the timer stops after 90 seconds, however, two crashes end the game. Since extra cars supply two crashes each, he can do well if he reaches 4,000. Unfortunately, the course keeps getting harder.

STRATEGIES

a. Always keep the gas pedal down except in bottlenecks (see Strategy h).

b. Get back onto the road right after a crash. Start in low gear, then shift permanently to high once you are going as fast as the other cars. If you start in high, you will probably get hit from behind.

c. Stay away from the side when you can; you don't want to decelerate or crash.

d. Be prepared for a puddle's effects when you see you are about to go through one.

e. Always keep on the alert for other cars. As soon as you see one, you should gauge in which direction it is drifting across the road and on which side you should pass it.

f. Be warned by sirens that you must look out for an ambulance coming from behind. As soon as it passes you, get behind it to avoid the cars on either side.

g. Night driving is hard, but stay in high gear and try to follow normal procedure. As soon as a car appears in your head-lights, judge whether it is a threat to you. If you decide it is, shift slightly away from it.

If you are hit near the end of a dark section, stay off the road until daylight. Otherwise, you might keep getting hit from behind and wasting precious time or cars, depending on how many points you have.

h. When you see the flashing bottleneck sign ahead, switch in-to low gear and move to the center of the road, avoiding the other cars. Once you are in the narrows, stay in low and use the gas pedal to regulate your speed, thus avoiding a crash.

26. SKY RAIDER

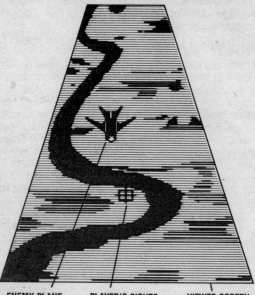

ENEMY PLANE   **PLAYER'S SIGHTS**   **VIEWER SCREEN**

CONTROLS

a. Combined steering wheel and thrust

b. FIRE button on right handle of wheel

SCORING

a. Tower: 350 points

b. Oil refinery: 450 points

c. Bridge: 450 points

d. City: 450 points

e. Enemy plane: 800 points

f. Extended play at 18,000 points

DANGERS

a. When the player's time runs out, the game ends.

OBSERVATIONS

a. Targets often appear on the viewer screen in clusters of three or four.

b. Pushing the steering wheel forward increases speed. A player flying fast cannot hit all the clustered targets for two reasons: air speed is so great that each target must be sighted and fired at as soon as it appears, and bombs cannot be dropped quickly enough to destroy all the targets in succession.

c. Sometimes, even a slow flier cannot shift his sight from one side of the screen to the other in time to destroy a target. He must then make a choice between sides.

d. Enemy planes are the most difficult targets: they appear at one upper corner of the screen and quickly travel to the opposite lower corner, where they disappear. By the time the unprepared player is ready to fire, the plane's course has usually taken it too close or too far over to hit. Planes do, however, appear in the same sequence every time.

STRATEGIES

a. Taking your air speed into account, fly fast only when the targets are few and far between. There is no bonus for speed, but you will score more points by destroying as many clusters as you can, and you must fly slowly over the clusters for maximum points.

b. Fire constantly! The mechanism permits a maximum of about two shots per second.

c. Although the targets appear in the same sequence every time, it's not necessary to memorize. This is a reflex game, and knowledge of the target sequence will not improve your score beyond a certain point.

d. Keep your eyes at the top of the screen; otherwise, your opportunity for reaction will be lessened. Know when you can turn to one target before the last explodes.

e. With practice, it is possible to develop a fast-slow-fire rhythm for single targets; use your shoulders.

f. Know your point values. If you see a tower on one side of the screen and another target across from it, you may not be able to hit both of them. Which will you go for? Not the tower.

g. The plane, of course, is the most important target of all. You can memorize the planes' appearances, but you will hit almost as many simply by shooting bombs constantly into the center of the screen; each plane must pass through the center in its course.

27. SPACE ZAP

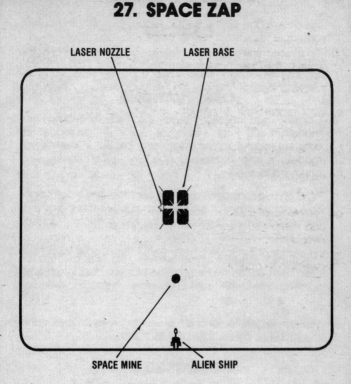

LASER NOZZLE   LASER BASE

SPACE MINE   ALIEN SHIP

CONTROLS

a. Four round panels for placing the laser nozzle

b. One FIRE panel

SCORING

a. Space mine: 250 points

b. Alien ship: 500 points

c. Attack satellite: 2,000 points

d. Bonus laser base every 75,000 points

DANGERS

a. If a space mine or attack satellite reaches the center of the screen, the laser base is destroyed.

OBSERVATIONS

a. Game-A-Tron licensed the game to Midway and has also manufactured it on its own. The Game-A-Tron model has different scoring and no attack satellites but, in the Midway model, the laser nozzle is dark against a dark background and hard to see.

b. An alien ship may appear at the center of any edge at any time and fire mines at the laser base until one or the other is destroyed. When the player destroys a ship, it vanishes, soon to be replaced by another.

c. The attack satellites come between bouts of battling the alien ships (in the Midway model). One comes each time, spiraling in from the edge until, unless it is zapped, it demolishes the laser base.

d. The game gets faster and faster until the laser base is constantly beset by ships from all four sides.

STRATEGIES

a. Keep your right hand close to the laser panels; gentle pressure is enough to relocate the laser nozzle. Fire constantly with your left hand, making seven shots per second your goal.

b. Watch the edges. SPACE ZAP requires even better peripheral vision than most video games.

c. Once the game is going, you won't have time to see whether you've hit a target or not. You'll just have to sense it, because you'll have more mines coming at you from all sides. Rhythm is very important, since you want the nozzle on one side only while you need it there, and you need it on three others simultaneously.

d. It works fairly well to shoot in a swift circle, top-right-bottom-left-top, reflexively completing one circuit each second or second and a half. Whatever you do, never stop firing.

e. When an attack satellite appears, fire in one direction fast enough and you will hit it.

f. Theoretically, you can play forever on one quarter once you get good enough, since you will keep getting extra bases every 75,000 points.

8

MISCELLANEOUS
GAMES

28. BATTLEZONE

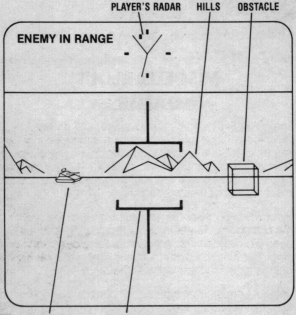

ENEMY TANK   PLAYER'S SIGHTS

CONTROLS

a. Two forward-back joysticks, one for the left tread and one for the right

b. FIRE button on right joystick

SCORING

a. Tank: 1,000 points

b. Missile: 2,000 points

c. Supertank: 3,000 points

d. Saucer: 5,000 points

e. Bonus tanks at 15,000 and 100,000 points

DANGERS

a. Collision with any missile destroys the player's tank.

b. Being shelled by any tank or supertank destroys the player's tank.

OBSERVATIONS

a. The screen depicts a plain bordered by distant hills. The plain is empty except for the player's tank, enemy armaments, and various geometric obstacles. The player can always see a few pyramids, cubes, and oblongs around him; if he drives past them, new ones materialize and grow more distinct as he approaches.

Pyramids and cubes can provide cover for the player, but the oblongs are low enough for him and his enemies to fire over. The obstacles do not destroy the player's tank on impact, but they do block its movements. All shells explode against the obstacles without effect.

b. Tanks, missiles, and supertanks appear one at a time somewhere within firing range of the player's tank. When one is destroyed, the next appears about two seconds later.

c. Above the large picture is a radar screen that shows the location of all enemies except saucers. The tank is always facing north on the screen.

d. The player can see everything in front of him in about a 40° arc. To shift his view, he must move his whole tank. Whenever he has an enemy in his sights, they change from a dim square to a bright X, so he can aim as accurately as possible.

The player can have only one shell on the screen at a time. If he misses, his shell takes over three seconds to detonate against the background hills.

To move straight forward or back, the player must move

both joysticks forward or back. Shifting the right one forward or back curves the tank forward or back and to the left; the left one, forward or back and to the right. If the player pushes one joystick all the way forward and pulls the other all the way back, the tank rotates in place.

e. The enemy tanks and supertanks make sounds when they shoot, and the warning of a missile's approach is unmistakable.

f. To the left of the radar appear three readouts:

1. A warning that there is an enemy within firing range

2. A warning that an object is blocking the player's movement

3. The direction of any enemy except saucers (left, right, ahead, or rear)

g. Like the player's, an enemy tank must move to shift its aim. It never fires unless it has the player in its sights, and always at least two seconds after its appearance. From then on, it is constantly turning slowly to face the player. It fires one shell at a time and shoots more frequently the closer it is to the player's tank.

When a pyramid or cube stands between the two tanks, the enemy will advance until it bumps against the obstacle, then back away to one side and drive off to the other, showing the player its vulnerable flank.

h. Supertanks move and shoot like ordinary ones, but somewhat faster.

i. Missiles descend from over the mountains in front of the player and try to ram his tank. The first visual sign of one is a short, crackling line on the horizon.

Missiles often come in pairs, one after the other; the first of the pair usually descends from top center. About one out of every five missiles descends from top right.

Once the missile is on the plain, it skitters back and forth before homing in on the tank; it skips over any obstacle in its path.

j. Saucers are no threat to the player, but they can contribute significantly to his score. They appear randomly and pursue random courses across the plain. If the player happens to catch sight of one, he can pursue it, but his more menacing enemies still threaten him.

Unlike his other adversaries, saucers do not explode to smithereens when hit; they merely glow for two seconds and then fade away.

k. As the game progresses, the player encounters more and more missiles and supertanks and fewer regular tanks.

STRATEGIES

a. Use the obstacles for protection, but bumping into one when you are trying to evade enemy fire can be deadly.

b. Whenever your tank or an enemy or both are destroyed, your eyes should shift to the radar to locate your next adversary.

c. The radar makes your survival possible, so don't ignore it.

d. You should almost never stand still. Between adversaries, alternate between forward left and forward right.

e. When you see from the readout that your enemy is on the plain but not in range, rotate toward it. Even if it is too far away and too faint for you to see, your sights will pinpoint it as soon as it enters them.

f. Listen for the sounds of missiles and tank shells. They may help you react more quickly.

g. If you watch the radar carefully, the most useful part of the additional readout will be the blockage warning. Because you will die if you can't maneuver freely, move away from whatever is blocking you as soon as possible.

h. If a tank is in front of you, follow one of two procedures:

1. Try to put an obstacle between yourself and the tank. Pick one and move toward it using just one joystick. The tank's shots will keep missing you as it turns to keep up.

   Once you are behind the pyramid or cube, wait while the tank approaches and then backs away to one side. At that point, blast it. While you wait, you can occupy your time by shooting at a saucer if you know where one is. They are good to chase even when you are not under cover, in fact, but do it carefully and evasively.

2. If you see no handy obstacles, approach the tank in a jerky zigzag pattern, keeping just to one side of the tank's line of fire. Pull up beside it; you won't be able to see it, but the radar will show it as a dot very close to center.

   Meanwhile, it will be turning to draw a bead on you. When you suddenly pull back both joysticks, you will catch it off guard. You will back up, it will come back into your sights, and you will be able to shoot as it turns back to face you.

i. If the radar shows a tank to your right or left, turn to face it with a curving advance—**not** by spinning in place. For the quickest pace ahead and to the left, keep the right joystick forward and move the left one forward every two seconds; ahead and to the right, vice versa. While it is firing and missing, it will come into your sights. You can then treat it as explained above.

j. If a tank appears behind you, quickly make a 45° to 90° turn, putting it to your right or left before it can shoot. Then use Strategy i.

   Never turn to face a tank by backing up to one side or the other. It's fine if it works, but why take the chance of hitting an obstacle and being shelled because you can't move?

k. It is best to hit a supertank on your first shot, since its speed makes each attempt dangerous.

l. When a missile appears at top center or top left, turn to the left a little. It will go back and forth, then home straight in on you. When it does, you have about a second to fire. Even if you miss, instantly moving full speed ahead will give you some chance of survival.

Conversely, turn slightly to the right when the missile approaches from top right. Once it gets a bead on you, you have only half a second to fire. If you miss, start getting your next tank ready.

29. CRAZY CLIMBER

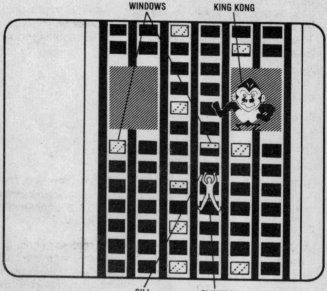

CONTROLS

CONTROLS

a. Two eight-directional joysticks, one to control each of the climber's hands

SCORING

a. Story in first building: 100 points

b. Story in second building: 150 points

c. Story in third building: 200 points, and so on

d. Bonus with each helicopter pickup

e. Extra climber at 30,000 points

DANGERS

a. Windows

b. Flowerpots and cans dropped by evil doctors

c. Girders

d. Condor

e. King Kong

f. Signs

OBSERVATIONS

a. The game has four buildings, each 200 stories high. Their names, in order, are Nichibutsu, Nichibutsu Leisure, Nichibutsu U.K. Ltd., and Nichibutsu U.S.A. Corp. (the originators of CRAZY CLIMBER, which is also licensed to Taito).

b. The climber can maneuver upward and sideways, but never downward. He must always avoid shut windows, since his hands rest on the sills and lose their grip whenever windows close on them. He must always have at least one hand securely placed in order not to fall.

c. The machine uses its voice synthesizer to produce the encouraging command, "Go for it!" It is programmed to do so whenever the climber has not moved for several seconds.

d. Except for windows, the waves of dangers listed above come only one at a time, and most are announced by recognizable musical themes. If one climber should happen to perish in the midst of a danger, that wave will be finished for the next climber, who must then face the next danger.

e. The bonus awaiting the climber at the roof is really a form of timer, since it decreases by 100 points with every ten seconds he spends climbing. He starts the first building with a bonus of 10,000 points, the second with a bonus of 20,000 points, and so on.

f. Evil doctors with red faces and fiendish grins appear at

points throughout the game to drop flowerpots only (on the first building) or flowerpots and cans from random windows.

It takes about two seconds for a doctor to appear, lean from his window, and drop his missile. One flowerpot will not harm the climber if he is holding on with both hands (he will just yell "OW!") but he will fall if he is climbing or if a window has closed on one hand when he is hit. Two simultaneous missiles will send a climber plummeting to his death, no matter how secure his grip is.

g. An evil doctor appearing at one of the climber's handholds and releasing a pot will cause the climber to fall.

h. The ledges between windows are safe from flowerpots but not from the girders tumbling down the second building and there'after.

i. If the player cannot dodge a deadly double bomb, holding both joysticks up occasionally saves the climber. Similarly, girders can often be withstood on the first sixteen floors of any building simply by jerking both joysticks downward. From the seventeenth floor up, dodging sideways is the only escape.

j. The condor makes two passes back and forth across the top of the screen during each of its appearances, ejecting three pairs of missiles in each crossing. A secure climber will not mind if one dropping hits his hand or shoulder, but a direct hit on his head or on his only entrenched hand will fell him.

k. King Kong leaps from side to side of the building, with only two columns of windows between his two perches. From his perch, he slams a hand onto a window in the nearer column every second, swatting whatever climber may be there. He switches sides every three or four seconds.

l. There is usually one column in which to escape the live wires snaking from the NICHIBUTSU sign. The CRAZY CLIMBER sign, although much narrower, crashes down for three floors, bounces a couple of times, then comes crashing down again, tearing off any climber in its path.

m. If the climber can catch the lucky balloon, not only will it lift him about ten floors, but it will raise his bonus score.

n. This is the sequence of events on the first building, excluding the ubiquitous windows:

   1. Evil doctors, one on the screen at a time

   2. Condor

   3. Evil Doctors, two at a time

   4. King Kong

   5. Evil Doctors, three at a time

   6. Roof and helicopter

o. This is the sequence of events on the second building:

   1. Girders, two at a time

   2. Evil doctors, three at a time

   3. Condor

   4. Girders, one at a time

   5. NICHIBUTSU sign

   6. Lucky balloon

   7. Roof and helicopter

p. This is the sequence of events for the third building:

   1. Girders, three at a time

   2. Evil doctors, three at a time

   3. Girders, one at a time

   4. Three to five CRAZY CLIMBER signs, depending on climber's speed—the faster, the fewer

   5. King Kong

6. Lucky balloon

7. Helicopter at roof

q. And this is the sequence for the fourth building:

1. Girders, four at a time

2. NICHIBUTSU sign

3. Condor, which now ejects four droppings at a time instead of two

4. Evil doctors, three at a time

5. Girders, one at a time

6. Building splits into two, with two lanes in each tower

7. Four to six CRAZY CLIMBER signs. If the player is in the right tower, he may escape, but it is all luck

8. Roof and helicopter, which transports the climber back to the base of the first building

STRATEGIES

a. Try to be constantly climbing, switching from column to column only when you have to. Remember the bonus!

b. There are two methods of climbing, each one better for certain situations. For best maneuverability under attack, keep both your hands in one column of windows. For speed between attacks, when windows are always closing above you and to the side, put your left hand in one column and your right hand in another, making it much easier to sidestep shut windows without pausing.

c. Disregard "Go for it!" Climb only when the time is right.

d. If trapped by closed windows, you have no choice but to grit your teeth and wait.

e. Anticipate upcoming dangers by knowing the sequences

listed in Observations n through q and listening for the musical themes.

f. React to the evil doctors either by dodging or by securing both hands. If a doctor appears where your hand is, you must jerk it away before he drops his pot. Try to stand still only when you have to.

g. If you are spreadeagled and a pot is hurtling towards one of your hands, pull it back to the ledge until the pot has passed.

h. From the seventeenth floor up, you must dodge girders as soon as they appear.

i. When the condor flies over you, dodge as soon as you think one of the droppings might hit your head.

j. Escaping King Kong is easy enough: climb to just below his hand and wait for him to switch to the other side. As soon as he does, climb like crazy.

k. There is nothing you can do about the CRAZY CLIMBER signs on the fourth building, so you might as well climb while you can for maximum points.

l. Try to catch the lucky balloon, but be alert if you do; it might set you down again at a window that's just closing.

30. MISSILE COMMAND

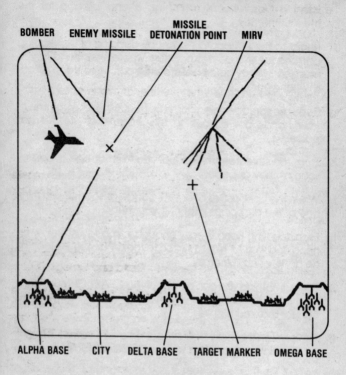

BOMBER   ENEMY MISSILE   MISSILE DETONATION POINT   MIRV

ALPHA BASE   CITY   DELTA BASE   TARGET MARKER   OMEGA BASE

CONTROLS

a. Trak-Ball

b. Three FIRE buttons, one for each missile base

SCORING

a. Missile: 25 points in first round

b. Bomber: 100 points in first round

c. Killer satellite: 100 points in first round

d. Smart missile: 125 points in first round

162

e. Bonus at end of each round

f. Bonus city every 10,000 points

DANGERS

a. Any missile destroys whatever city or missile base it hits.

b. When the player runs out of cities, the game ends.

OBSERVATIONS

a. The player starts each round with each of his three missile bases fully equipped with ten missiles. From left to right, they are Alpha Base, Delta Base, and Omega Base. Delta Base's missiles are faster than those of the two side bases.

b. The operator can choose to allot the player four to seven cities, but the usual number is six, three between Alpha and Delta Bases and three between Delta and Omega Bases.

c. The Trak-Ball, patented by Atari, works the same way as the one in CENTIPEDE, but it controls a target mark shaped like a plus sign (+). When the player presses a FIRE button, the designated base launches a missile at wherever the + is. Even when the + moves on, it leaves behind an X.

When the missile reaches the X, it detonates. The cloud of the explosion expands for about a second, reaching a diameter of over an inch, and then takes another second to shrink to nothingness. Any enemy that touches this cloud is destroyed. The player can have up to eight missiles on the screen at once.

d. At the beginning of each round, missiles begin falling from the top of the screen. If allowed, each one will fall straight to a target below, either a city or a missile base.

Some of them are MIRVs, capable of splitting into any number of missiles at any point. When they do, each splinter missile has the power and value of an ordinary one. The number of possible splits is limited, because each round has a fixed number of missiles. Most rounds consist of two waves; the more missiles split in the first wave, the fewer can fall from the top in the second.

e. From Round Two on, bombers and killer satellites fly straight across the screen from the right or the left. When one exits or is destroyed, the next soon appears at the same level, although the level varies from round to round.

If a bomber or killer satellite is not destroyed, it may send down missiles, even MIRVs.

f. The first smart missile appears in Round Six, and the diamond-shaped menaces become more and more numerous. A smart missile is well named, since it avoids any missile that detonates more than a quarter-inch below it. It can move to either side but not back up, and it cannot remain at the same level for long without descending.

Smart missiles, unlike ordinary ones, always head for sites that have not yet been destroyed, so they usually cause damage when not stopped. However, the player cannot lose more than three cities in one round.

g. When any missile, bomber, or satellite is destroyed, its explosion can destroy others in turn.

h. There are never more than eight enemy missiles on the screen at once.

i. When the last enemy missile is launched, a beep signals that no more will come. When the last enemy missile is destroyed, the + disappears until the beginning of the next round. Then the player receives a bonus of 5 points for each missile and 100 for each city he has left.

j. In the third and fourth rounds, every score, including the bonuses at the end, is multiplied by two; in the fifth and sixth, by three; in the seventh and eighth, by four; in the ninth and tenth, by five; and from the eleventh on, by six. Unfortunately, more and more missiles fall faster and faster as their values increase, and up to 13 or 14 smart missiles fall in a single round.

k. The more cities you are allowed, the easier it is to score points, because of the bonus you receive for each one at the end of each round; on the other hand, you have more sites to protect.

l. Not all operators set 10,000 as the score needed for another city, although most do. Whatever they pick, something special happens at 800,000 points over their selection. Usually at 810,000 points, the player receives a limitless number of cities, so he can devote all his energy to scoring points and none to surviving. Unfortunately, The bonanza ceases when he turns the machine over at 1,000,000.

STRATEGIES

a. Develop accuracy with the Trak-Ball. Once you get the feel of it, you should be able to maneuver anywhere without thinking or even looking.

b. You don't have time to view the results of your shots. Just put the + where you want it, press FIRE, and move on to the next target.

c. It is rarely a good idea to press more than one FIRE button at a time, since it usually means the waste of a missile. You should do it only when you know you will need two explosions in one spot, one soon after the other.

d. After the first round, you must aim in front of a missile to destroy it. If possible, shoot with one of the two bases nearer the enemy missile, preferably Alpha or Omega, so that you can save your quick Delta shots for emergencies.

e. MIRVs are desirable in early rounds, since they branch out so slowly that you can eliminate five or six misiles with only two or three missiles. In later rounds, though, the missiles travel so fast that you don't want them to split, since you might not have time to react. The sooner you can destroy MIRVs, therefore, the better. Since they look the same as regular missiles, try to exterminate everything.

f. Destroy bombers and killer satellites at the earliest opportunity, for two reasons:

1. Because the missiles they drop start lower, they are more dangerous. You want to prevent them from falling at all.

2. The faster you shoot bombers and satellites, the more can appear in each round, and the more points you can score.

g. Listen for the beep that signals the last missle of the round. If you destroy what you think is the last but your + does not disappear, there are more coming. Be ready for them.

h. To destroy a smart missile, wait until it is near the ground, position the + just beneath it, and fire. If you launch a quick Delta Base missile, your chances of success are the best possible.

i. Once the missiles get going really fast, it is very difficult to pick them off individually. Here is the technique known as "doing a spread" or "making a wall":

1. As soon as the round starts, position the + a little below center on one side of the screen and move slowly across, pressing FIRE eight times as you do. If you are moving to the right, fire from Omega; if to the left, from Alpha.

2. You will have two missiles left there when you are done. If you spaced the shots well, the first wave of enemies will be met by a solid wall of nuclear cloud in which even MIRVs will perish.

3. Before your first missiles detonate, shoot the first bomber or satellite.

4. Perfect walls are rare, so look for holes in yours and pick off the few survivors from Delta Base.

5. You know that the second wave is coming, so repeat the whole process. This time, though, move in the other direction, and fire from the base in the other corner.

   Delta Base will have enough missiles to pick off stragglers and smart missiles, while you can use the corner bases for bombers and satellites.

You will need to build your walls lower as the missiles move faster, but they will never move too fast.

j. Rounds occasionally start with one smart missile followed by a horde of regular ones. When that occurs, simply lower your + slightly from its usual level, pause, and then build a wall. The smart missile will not survive. Because the wall is low, you must deal with lucky survivors quickly.

k. Like ASTEROIDS, MISSILE COMMAND has a loophole for long-term players: after you have scored about 115,000 points, you don't need more than one city at a time, so you can let the others go. One is easier to protect than six, so you'll have more time for the serious business of shooting the many smart missiles, whose scores alone are enough for a new city every round.

For the first wall, fire from the base farthest from your city. Afterwards, you will have only half the screen to protect—except for all the smart missiles. This simple stratagem has already enabled players to score over 50,000,000 points on one quarter.

9

OFF-MACHINE EXERCISES

Physical adeptness is essential to implementing your strategies. In your spare time, you and a friend can work on improving hand-eye coordination, peripheral vision, finger strength, and tempo control. The exercises can be enjoyably challenging and will sharpen skills just as effectively as the first few quarters you put into a game you want to learn. They should be adjusted to the player's abilities and needs.

When playing arcade games for any amount of time, remember to keep your back and neck relaxed but straight, thus avoiding stiffness and cricks.

Hands

You will accomplish wonders by training your hands to react as quickly as possible to visual stimuli.

Exercise: have your friend drop a pen from various heights, from four to seven feet. Stand a foot away and keep your right hand at your side until you see the pen drop; then, reach and catch it before it hits the ground (see diagram). The different heights are necessary to prevent your relying more on reflex than on actual coordination. When you have made ten clean catches in a row with each hand, let your friend try.

Eyes

Some games use sound effects to warn the player of danger; a topnotch player, however, must also be alert to the slightest flicker of movement in any part of the screen and be able to analyze all visual data without shifting focus.

Exercise: have your friend stand three feet from you at about two o'clock. Stare straight ahead while he holds up a random number of fingers; call out how many you see. If you are correct on the first try, have your friend move more and more to your right side, until you make a wrong guess. He should then maintain this position. Keeping your head **and** eyes straight ahead, try to concentrate enough to answer correctly five times in a row. Repeat the exercise on your left side, then switch with him.

This exercise is designed to strengthen and hone your natural peripheral vision. Often, what you see "out of the corner of your eye" can mean life or death on screen.

Fingers

Anyone who has played games using button controls knows how essential digital skill can be. Fingers must be strong and limber, since sustained play produces pain and slowness in the joints of unprepared fingers.

Exercise: wrap the fingers of your right hand tightly around a pen. Then extend the forefinger and begin to rotate it clockwise around a doorknob. You should start slowly, at about 30 revolutions per minute (rpm), retaining your grip on the pen and keeping your wrist as stationary as possible. Try never to touch the doorknob and never to wander more than half an inch from it (see diagram).

If your finger hurts slightly, it should: the muscles are being stretched and loosened. Now accelerate the rotations to 60 rpm. If you can hold your orbit for one minute, you are doing well.

Now alternate between clockwise and counterclockwise motion, starting slowly and increasing speed each time. Finally, repeat the entire process with your left hand.

Pulling each finger back as far as it will go and keeping it there for ten seconds before playing will loosen a different, but also important, set of muscles. Since one quarter can buy you hours of play, you should stretch your finger muscles before beginning any session, to be sure that cramps and pains will not hamper your enjoyment.

Tempo

Advanced play in all video games requires a firm command of timing; often this mastery involves the ability to fall into various rhythms inherent to the games. Two examples are the move-stop-shoot rhythm so crucial in SPACE INVADERS-type games, and the thrust-turn-shoot rhythm of most ASTEROIDS-type games (see Chapter 3).

Exercise: try to tap a pen on a table at intervals of **exactly** one second for 30 seconds, having a friend time you. Once you have accomplished that, move up to intervals of two seconds for a minute, then of three seconds for a minute and a half, and so on. Intervals of seven seconds are the most difficult you are likely to need for developing sufficient rhythmic skill.

10

THE TV CONNECTION

Many arcade players tend to look down on home video games. They say the graphics and sound effects are less sophisticated, the games are less challenging and the technology is less advanced.

Home video can be as difficult or more so, if the player wishes; moreover, the technology isn't behind at all. Both industries use space effectively: if a game cartridge costs about a tenth of what an arcade game does and is much smaller, players cannot expect the bulky and elaborate circuits of an arcade game, or even the same sound and image production.

Home video games deliver everything they promise, including some advantages over their coin-op counterparts: privacy, unlimited play, and the player's choice of time and place.

America's five major home game collections are Atari's Video Computer System, Mattel's Intellivision, Magnavox's Odyssey^2, Astrovision's Bally Professional Arcade, and Fairchild's Channel F. Another company, Activision, has also produced ten excellent cartridges for the Atari system so far.

The systems are all educational, sports simulation, or arcade-type games. The educational ones usually improve mathematical ability, spelling, computer fluency, or memory. Some reproduce such popular and useful games as Nim, Concentration, Mastermind, Simon, and hangman, pitting players against the computer or each other. You can practice or play backgammon, casino games, chess, checkers, Othello, or bridge whenever you feel like it.

If you're in the mood for electronic athletics, you can participate quite realistically in any sport from Alpine skiing to football, from drag racing to bowling.

Then there are the arcade games. Many are original games, often with the usual themes: tanks, space battle, video pinball, etc. Some, however, are versions of well-known arcade games, such as ASTEROIDS, BREAKOUT, CLOWNS, CRASH, MISSILE COMMAND, NIGHT DRIVER, SPACE INVADERS, and WARLORDS.

Don't expect exactly what you get in the arcade; the MISSILE COMMAND program, for instance, features one base with 30 missiles instead of three with 10 each. But the fundamentals are the same, so most of the strategies for the arcade games still apply.

The graphics and sounds are a little less exciting, but the TV versions offer compensations. SPACE INVADERS, for example, has only 36 invaders in each screen instead of 55, but it offers many different skill levels. The player can choose variations such as curving missiles, shifting bunkers, or invisible invaders, whichever strike his fancy.

All in all, if you like video games, you should definitely take home video into consideration. Once you make the initial investment for equipment, new cartridges are available at low prices. You or your friends or family can play exciting, challenging, imaginative games.

APPENDIX:
SOME OF THE
MAJOR MANUFACTURERS

Amstar Electronics Corp.
1960 W. North Lane
Phoenix, AZ 85021
(602) 997-5931

Amusement Systems
1202 West Central Blvd.
Orlando, FL 32805
(305) 422-5199

Atari, Inc.
1265 Borregas Ave.
Sunnyvale, CA 94086
(408) 745-2500

Centuri, Inc.
245 West 74th Place
Hialeah, FL 33014
(305) 558-5200

Cinematronics, Inc.
1466 Pioneer Way
El Cajon, CA 92020
(714) 440-2933

Data East, Inc.
470 Gianni St.
Santa Clara, CA 95050
(408) 727-4490

Elcon Industries
2715 Nakota
Royal Oak, MI 48073
(313) 549-1140

Electro-Sport, Inc.
17842 Cowan
Irvine, CA 92714
(714) 979-1875

Exidy, Inc.
390 Java Drive
Sunnyvale, CA 94086
(408) 734-9410

Ferncrest Distributors, Inc.
66 Illinois Ave.
Warwick, RI 02888
(401) 737-1771

Game-A-Tron Corp.
931 West Main St.
New Britain, CT 06050
(203) 223-2760

Game Plan, Inc.
1515 W. Fullerton Ave.
Addison, IL 60101
(312) 628-8200

D. Gottlieb & Co.
165 West Lake St.
Northlake, IL 60164
(312) 562-7400

Gremlin Industries, Inc.
8401 Aero Drive
San Diego, CA 92123
(714) 277-8700

Hoei International, Inc.
9000 Sunset Blvd.
Los Angeles, CA 90069
(213) 278-7090

Meyco Games, Inc.
650 Vacqueros Ave., Unit D
Sunnyvale, CA 94086
(408) 245-1603

Midway Manufacturing Co.
10750 W. Grand Ave.
Franklin Park, IL 60131
(312) 452-5200

Myimpa Export, Inc.
10 Keith Way
Hingham, MA 02043
(617) 749-8198

Namco America, Inc.
343 Gibraltar Drive
Sunnyvale, CA 94086
(408) 745-7600

Nanao Corporation
1148 Franklin Rd. SE
Marietta, GA 30067
(404) 952-9777

Nichibutsu U.S.A. Corp.
1815 W. 205th St.,
  Unit No. 302
Torrance, CA 90501
(213) 327-5982

Nintendo of America, Inc.
1107 Broadway, Suite 1420
New York, NY 10010
(212) 741-3247

Omni Video, Inc.
66 Illinois St.
Warwick, RI 02888
(401) 738-5065

Rock-Ola Mfg. Corp.
800 N. Kedzie
Chicago, IL 60651
(312) 638-7600

Sega Enterprises, Inc.
2029 Century Park East,
  Suite 2920
Los Angeles, CA 90067
(213) 557-1700

Segasa/Sonic
430 N. Maple Dr.
Beverly Hills, CA 90210
(213) 550-7608

Stern Electronics, Inc.
1725 Diversey Pkwy.
Chicago, IL 60614
(312) 935-4600

Taito America Corp.
1256 Estes Ave.
Elk Grove Village, IL 60007
(312) 981-1000

U.S. Billiards, Inc.
243 Dixon Ave.
Amityville, NY 11701
(516) 842-4242

Universal U.S.A., Inc.
3250 Victor St.
Santa Clara, CA 95050
(408) 727-4591

Williams Electronics, Inc.
3401 N. California Ave.
Chicago, IL 60618
(312) 267-2240

Home Video Games

Activision, Inc.
3255-2 Scott Blvd.
Santa Clara, CA 95051
(408) 727-7770

Astrovision
6400 Busch Blvd., Ste. 225
Columbus, OH 43229
(614) 885-0130

Atari, Inc.
1265 Borregas Ave.
Sunnyvale, CA 94086
(408) 745-2500

Magnavox Consumer Elec. Corp.
P.O. Box 6950
Knoxville, Tennessee 37914
(615) 521-4332

Mattel, Inc.
5150 Rosecrans Ave.
Hawthorne, CA 90250
(213) 978-5150

Zircon International, Inc.
   (Fairchild's distributor)
475 Vandell Way
Campbell, CA 95008
(408) 866-4500

We Deliver!

And So Do These Bestsellers.

☐	20230	**THE LAST MAFIOSO: The Treacherous** World of Jimmy Fratianno	$3.95
☐	20296	**THE COMING CURRENCY COLLAPSE** by Jerome F. Smith	$3.95
☐	14998	**LISTEN AMERICA!** by Jerry Falwell	$3.50
☐	20700	**THE RIGHT STUFF** Tom Wolfe	$3.95
☐	20229	**LINDA GOODMAN'S SUN SIGNS**	$3.95
☐	14391	**THE THIRD WAVE** by Alvin Toffler	$3.95
☐	01341	**NEWBORN BEAUTY: A complete beauty,** health, and energy guide to the nine months of pregnancy, and the nine months after by W. Gates & Gail Meckel	$9.95
☐	20483	**WEALTH AND POVERTY** by George Gilder	$3.95
☐	20198	**BOOK OF PREDICTIONS** by Wallechinsky & Irving Wallace	$3.95
☐	20506	**WHEN LOVERS ARE FRIENDS** by Merle Shain	$2.50
☐	13101	**THE BOOK OF LISTS #2** by I. Wallace, D. Wallechinsky, A. & S. Wallace	$3.50
☐	14075	**THE COMPLETE SCARSDALE MEDICAL DIET** by Herman Tarnover & S. Baker	$3.50
☐	05003	**THE GREATEST SUCCESS IN THE WORLD** by Og Mandino (A Large Format Book)	$6.95
☐	20434	**ALL CREATURES GREAT AND SMALL** by James Herriot	$3.95
☐	14017	**THE SIMPLE SOLUTION TO RUBIK'S CUBE** by Nour	$1.95
☐	14331	**THE THIRD WAVE** by Alvin Toffler	$3.95
☐	20621	**THE PILL BOOK** by Dr. Gilbert Simon & Dr. Harold Silverman	$3.95
☐	01352	**THE PEOPLE'S ALMANAC #3** by David Wallechinsky & Irving Wallace A Large Format Book	$10.95
☐	14500	**GUINNESS BOOK OF WORLD RECORDS—** 19th Ed. by McWhirter	$3.50

Buy them at your local bookstore or use this handy coupon for ordering:

Bantam Books, Inc., Dept. NFB, 414 East Golf Road, Des Plaines, Ill. 60016

Please send me the books I have checked above. I am enclosing $_____
(please add $1.00 to cover postage and handling). Send check or money order
—no cash or C.O.D.'s please.

Mr/Mrs/Miss_____

Address_____

City_____State/Zip_____

NFB—1/82

Please allow four to six weeks for delivery. This offer expires 6/82.